WORK
IN THE FUTURE
ALTERNATIVES
TO
UNEMPLOYMENT

John Osmond

THORSONS PUBLISHING GROUP
Wellingborough, Northamptonshire

Rochester, Vermont

First published 1986

© JOHN OSMOND 1986

For Tomos Rhys

British Library Cataloguing in Publication Data

Osmond, John
   Work in the future: alternatives to
   unemployment.
   1. Subculture
   I. Title
   306'.1   HM73

ISBN 0-7225-1245-7

Printed and bound in Great Britain

WORK
IN THE FUTURE

Shows how many of the main trends in the economy point to
fewer jobs in the future, and examines how a variety of
communities, groups and individuals are seeking alternatives
to unemployment.

Contents

Photography

All pictures are by the author, with the exception of p. 37 — Terence Soanes (Cardiff) Ltd Photography, p. 47 — Caroline Weedon, p. 59 — Greater London Enterprise Board and p. 20, p. 86 and p. 109 — HTV Ltd.

Foreword

Theophrastus Paracelsus, the first physician to turn medicine from quackery into science, came to the conclusion that 'everything is poison; it all depends on the quantity'. He spoke of drugs and healing plants. But the principle applies also to all other things we use to improve the human condition: technology, business, wealth, leisure, government, states. Below a given point their increase in quantity and growth solves our problems. Above it, it creates and aggravates them. A measured dose of pain-killers kills pain. An overdose kills us. Growth of and within a community enhances the quality of life of the individual. With the greater variety it offers, it turns us into fuller human beings. Overgrowth destroys it, degrading the individual to the statistical cog-wheel position of an average person who, as Ortega y Gasset put it, 'is to history what sea-level is to geography' — an entity without sex, colour, class, race, creed, status, or height.

Nowhere is the poisonous effect of social overgrowth more evident than in the field of employment. For every arithmetic expansion beyond optimum size is accompanied by a geometric increase in complexities of such magnitude that only the most advanced technology is capable of satisfying the multiplying post-optimal survival requirements of a community. But the more advanced a technology, the more it must resort to forms of energy which, besides pilfering the world's resources and polluting our visual and physical environment, are so efficient that they smother us not only with mountains of beef, butter, powdered milk and cheese, but also with mountains of unemployed workers as well as the armies and guns necessary to liquidate them like King Cadmus' dragon-teeth soldiers through mutual saulghter. No wonder a leader of an overgrown power such as President Reagan might come to the conclusion that Armageddon is impending and, according to his son's, Ron Jr., lively imagination, in due course command one of his generals: 'Tell your boys to give those keys a crank, then high-tail it up to Camp David. Nancy is mixing up a pitcher of margaritas. We are going to circle the lawn chairs and watch the whole show from the back porch' (*The Observer*, 6 April 1986). All Gorbachov would do differently is to order vodka instead of margaritas.

Militarism is therefore not, as Marx has it, a consequence of profit-seeking, market-expanding capitalism. It is the consequence of cancerously overgrown societies demanding the sort of advanced technology that is capable not only of satisfying their astronomically swollen survival requirements but also of producing such quantities of surplus manpower that the only alternative to letting it rot in idleness and crime is to sponge it up in the infinitely expandable area of bureaucratic and military activities. All this amounts to is not abolishing unemployment but hiding it under a screen of medals, gun licenses, titles, and rank.

This means that none of the conventionally offered alternative solutions to the ever increasing technological unemployment of our time, with all it entails in the gradual militarization, criminalization and destruction of the human mission, is a real alternative: neither the further advance in social integration or technology, nor a switchover from capitalism to socialism, from old to young, from Rome to Mecca, from Reagan to Gorbachov, from Thatcher to Benn, from Murdoch to Dean. They may differ in accents and the use of terms. But they all continue to walk — beer, vodka, gin, or margarita in hand — the same road of hope and glory towards the blasphemous unity of a Tower-of-Babel society that has failed whenever it was attempted not so much because the road was wrong as because the hope-and-glory addicts kept pursuing it too far. You don't want to reach the North Pole merely because the needle of the compass keeps on pointing in its direction even when you have reached the limits of the inhabitable Earth.

The real alternative when the road begins to freeze up underneath one's feet is therefore not going ahead or choosing a different road to push further, but turning back — from a stiflingly unified to the sparkle of a diversified world; from the unbalanced congealed blocks of great powers to a self-balancing system of loosely associated dynamic small states; from multi-national corporations to local co-operatives; from advanced technology that kills work to intermediate technology that creates it; from the cosmic force of nuclear power capable of building atom bombs to the spiritual and physical force of muscle power capable of building cathedrals in marble, taverns in brick, and shepherd's dwellings in the magnificence of Cotswold stone; from bureaucratic centralism which caused Kafka to say: 'the chains of mankind consist of office forms', to devolution, or as Ioan Bowen Rees, the Chief Executive of Gwynedd County would put it, from centralism writ large to centralism writ small considering that even a small body can thrive only on a single head; from huge capital-intensive to small labour-intensive production units which absorb unemployed surplus labour on that ground alone but, like the human person, are economical only in a society of limited size just as pedestrian power is economical only in a city of limited extent, or a row boat within the limits of a small body of water.

This is the ecological approach to the solution of the otherwise intractable problem of contemporary vast-scale unemployment. Showing the way to the use of the full variety of complementary resources existing not in distant corners of the world but lying around in everybody's immediate neighbourhood, it permits even the poorest to gain height by building from the bottom up. Henry Klumb, the great tropical architect, demonstrated this in his luxurious Puerto Rican home when he told the advice-seeking leaders of the tiny Caribbean island state of Anguilla after their secession in 1967 from lavishly aid-assisted St Kitts: 'There is not an ounce of material in my house which you do not find also in the lowliest slum hut. All you need for raising your living standards is taste and will. And both are free.' By contrast, the academic classroom approach, forever trying to build from the top down, loses height with every step and yet has the greatest difficulty reaching the base for the simple reason that from its majestic altitude it cannot see where it is located.

For all this: what Sir Herbert Read said of buildings, that they 'begin on the ground, not in an office', applies, as John Osmond demonstrates so masterfully in the panoramic survey he offers in his new book, *Work in the Future*, also in all other fields of human endeavour. He argues his plea for a return from large to small scale, from governmental to local, co-operative, and individual initiative, with concisely formulated philosophical statements backed and illustrated by an array of fascinating figures. But most importantly he offers detailed descriptions of many of the almost staggering number of experiments and self-help projects in individual and co-operative re-employment which have successfully been carried out by such 'barefoot' economists as Guy Dauncey or Manfred Max-Neef in all corners of the world where the conventional approaches have led to nothing but more unemployment, more crime, more drug addiction, more terrorism, more despair. As an Alaskan tavern song puts it: 'Loafing all day, loafing all night, Nothing to do but pick a fight' — another illustration of the militarizing effect not of capitalist doctrines but of unemployment.

Because of the concrete measures it proposes and the examples it gives for creating work bootstrap fashion through direct, independent, neighbourhood-inspired action, *Work in the Future* offers so much practical ground-level guidance that it should have a market of readers, if not of buyers, in all the more than three million workers who are at this juncture unemployed in Great Britain alone. They might find themselves back at a job before being half-way through with the book. But even ambitious professionals might soften to its ideas considering that, after alternating for years between Leftists and Rightists, the most recent (1985) Nobel Prize in economics has for the first time been conferred on a Smallist, Professor Franco Modigliani of the Massachussetts Institute of Technology, for climbing not still higher up the ivory tower but for bringing the subject back from its shrouded cosmic altitude to the base from which Aristotle started it 2,350 years ago — the study of the household, which was the original meaning of the term economics to begin with.

As to myself, I have learned a great deal from reading John Osmond's newest book, as I have from his earlier work on *The Centralist Enemy* and his more general volume on *Alternatives* which accompanied his 1985 HTV series of documentary films. Acquainting me with the unexpectedly wide range of new literature on the subject as well as with the great number and success of small-scale local work-creating experiments in the midst of a sea of sterile costly mergers and conventional failures, it has not only reawakened my old ambition to initiate a long-planned film on *The Household Economics of Manning Farrell* to show how much can be done with how little, and what values can be created by recycling waste; it has also restored a glimmer of hope that the world may after all not yet have reached the vodka-margarita stage of terminal collapse which has been predicted first for 1984 and more recently for 1999.

But to strengthen this glimmer of hope, it is imperative to realize that today's field of alternative solutions is considerably narrower than before. The survival choice is no longer between left and right, or young and old. As a modern Hamlet might put it after reading Ivan Illich, Josef Haid, Hazel Henderson, Fritjof Kapra, Helena Norberg-Hodge, John Papworth, Fritz Schumacher, or John Osmond: 'To Be Small or Not to Be at All, *that* is the Question' of a time in danger to succumb to the cancer of giantism.

Leopold Kohr
The Cabin
Aberystwyth
April 1986

Preface

The idea that there is a *New Economics,* as an integrated alternative to traditionally understood conventional economics, emerged slowly during the writing of this book. That, in itself, is significant since it is another expression of the truth that the initiatives described herein are each a spontaneous and evolving response to particular circumstances.

Taken as a whole, however, they can be seen as sharing the same values in common. Nevertheless, the essence of the New Economics is that they are not handed down from above, but worked out in practice, from the bottom up.

This is a companion volume to *Alternatives* that I wrote with my colleague Angela Graham and which was published by Thorsons during 1984. Our comment then applies equally to this volume: 'We have been fascinated to discover that just beneath the surface of society in Britain today is evolving a whole new fabric . . . and it appears to us as an evolutionary process: the new growing within the faded structures of the old.'

Much of the information in this book is based on a documentary series *Working Alternatives,* broadcast by HTV Wales on the network during the summer of 1985. I should like to thank all my colleagues who worked on the programme, but particularly Jane Taylor who undertook much of the early research, and Michael W. Esthop, my film director, who provided a sceptical yet encouraging foil for my enthusiasm.

John Osmond

1. The New Economics

As technological change accelerates, economics is now merely
backing us into the future looking through the rear-view mirror.
— Hazel Henderson, speaking at the
1985 Other Economic Summit.

The Old Economics operates on the principle that people act
solely on the basis of self-interest, narrowly conceived in terms
of immediate material gain; the New Economics insists that that
self-interest has now become the wider interest of the ecological
balance of the planet. The Old Economics clings to the belief
that a return to full employment based on economic growth is
still possible; the New Economics declares that we have to re-
define our idea of work to embrace more than conventionally
paid employment and that growth relying on the depletion of
non-renewable resources is no longer an option. The language
of the Old and New Economics emphasizes the contrast. In place
of 'economic progress', 'industrial modernization', and 'growing
Gross National Product', the New Economics substitutes such
phrases as 'quality of life', 'human potential' and 'global ecological
balance'.

The hinge around which the argument between the Old and
New Economics turns is mass unemployment. Is it a temporary
or permanent phenomenon? Will the unemployment curve
retreat, stabilize, or continue inexorably upwards?

The conventional view is that past experience of booms and
slumps suggests that the present recession will be followed by
recovery; that new technology will generate new jobs to replace
the old; and that the windfall of North Sea oil will tide Britain

over the painful transition period into the next century.

The alternative view is that we are entering a new economic phase in which the comfortable certainties of the Old Economics just do not apply. In their book *The Collapse of Work,* published in 1979, Clive Jenkins and Barrie Sherman forecast that in twenty five years from then the number of people employed in mining and quarrying in Britain would fall by 24 per cent, in the coal and petroleum industries by 32 per cent, in the food, drink and tobacco industries by 40 per cent, in metal manufacture by 47 per cent, in shipbuilding by 60 per cent and in the textile industry by 74 per cent. Only in professional and scientific employment was there forecast an increase — of 2 per cent. Given these predictions, which in 1979 might have appeared apocalyptic but which six years later have a ring of veracity conditioned by experience, what comfort can we take in the conventional view that technological development will eventually re-employ those it is currently throwing out of work? Mike Cooley, technology director with the Greater London Enterprise Board and pioneer of the concept of socially useful production discussed in chapter 5, put it thus:

> We're going to see more and more people displaced by machines, both manual workers and white collar workers. When the multi-national entrepreneurs talk about the workerless factory they do actually mean that. And when they talk about that being followed by the workerless office, they mean that as well. So, therefore, I don't regard as alarmist predictions within the EEC that, by about 1988, even if we can maintain the present growth rate, we will have 20 million people out of work compared with about 12 or 13 million in 1985.
>
> We are moving towards having, on the one hand, a small elite of people working for the multi-national companies with medicare, international travel, and high salaries and, on the other hand, a vast number of people driven back to a kind of primitive, survival, therapeutic type of existence within communities where they will have no bargaining power in the conventional sense which we experienced it in the 30 years following World War II.

When Jenkins and Sherman forecast a collapse of work in 1979 the numbers unemployed in Britain had hovered around the 1.5 million mark for four years. In the next four years the official figure doubled to pass three million. The real figure was probably more

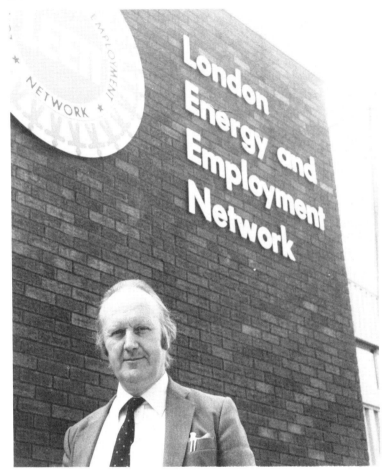

● Mike Cooley, technology director with the Greater London Enterprise Board: 'When the multi-national entrepreneurs talk about the workerless factory they do actually mean that . . .'

than four million if manipulation of the unemployment statistics, the exclusion of married women ineligible for supplementary benefit, and 400,000 mainly young people on temporary employment schemes were taken into account. Of course, the world trade recession and a government committed to a monetarist attack on inflation exacerbated the situation. But it is impossible to escape the evidence that investment and technological change underlie the displacement of swathes of previously secure workers. Listing just a few of the developments in the mid-1980s makes the point. Rolls Royce invested in a new automated production line in Derby, increasing productivity by 200 per cent and reducing unit labour costs by 20 per cent. A three-man shift now produces what used to take thirty men. In Liverpool, although Plessey expanded production of components for the new System X telephone exhanges, the workforce lost 825 out of 3,260 jobs. Between 1980 and 1984 Austin Rover increased productivity from 5.98 to 14.22 cars per man — and the workforce was cut by 20,000.

These examples do not touch on the impact of the micro-electronic and computer revolution, explored in chapter 6, which will be even more profound. Indeed, if the future predicted by Mike Cooley entails a two-class society, those with and those without work, there is likely to be a further sub-division within the fortunate group having access to paid employment. There will be a minority of high-paid workers, largely professional people in the high technology information sector, with the majority in the rest of the service sector — catering, hotels, tourism, insurance administration and the leisure industries generally, areas where there is likely to be growth, but of relatively poorly paid jobs.

A Holistic Approach

It is in response to such predictions, and in reaction to the threat that large-scale and long-term unemployment will become a permanent feature of the landscape, that the New Economics emerged in the 1980s. The theoretical foundations for it were already well prepared, however, by the work of two political economists and philosophers, E. F. Schumacher and Leopold Kohr. Between them they had developed over the previous thirty years the ideas of co-operation, appropriate size and technology, and ecological sensitivity that are the central preoccupations of the New Economics. It is right to describe Schumacher and Kohr as *political* economists since, unlike most theorists and, for that matter, practitioners, of the Old Economics, they give priority to politics over economics — to human relationships over production, distribution and exchange. In his *Small is Beautiful* whose sub-title, significantly, is *A Study of Economics as if People Mattered,* Schumacher summarizes his critique of the Old Economics by exposing the poverty of its reliance on the profit motive:

In the current vocabulary of condemnation there are few words as final and conclusive as the word *unecomonic*. If an activity has been branded as uneconomic, its right to existence is not merely questioned but energetically denied. Anything that is found to be an impediment to economic growth is a shameful thing, and if people cling to it, they are thought of as either saboteurs or fools. Call a thing immoral or ugly, soul-destroying or a degradation of man, a peril to the peace of the world or to the well-being of future generations; as long as you have not shown it to be *uneconomic* you have not really questioned its right to exist, grow and prosper.

And, as Schumacher goes on to point out, what is especially revealing, is the meaning that the Old Economics attaches to *uneconomic:*

Something is uneconomic when it fails to earn an adequate profit in terms of money. The method of economics does not and cannot, produce any other meaning . . . Society, or a group or an individual within society, may decide to hang on to an activity or asset for *non-economic reasons* — social, aesthetic, moral or political — but this does in no way alter its *uneconomic* character. The judgement of economics, in other words, is an extremely *fragmentary* judgement; out of the large number of aspects which in real life have to be seen and judged together before a decision can be taken, economics supplies only one — whether a thing yields a money profit to those who undertake it or not.

This, then, is the main thrust of the Old Economics. In contrast, the New Economics tempers the requirements of economic growth, enterprise and profit with their impact on the environment, with a co-operative as opposed to a competitive spirit, and with communal as opposed to individual benefit in mind. In short, the New Economics takes a holistic view in accord with an appreciation that the planet must be treated as a single ecological system. At the same time, the New Economics is extremely practical. It starts from the bottom up and stresses the importance of the local economy where problems are most manageable. In this the New Economics owes its greatest debt to Leopold Kohr whose work in the 1950s, most notably his book *The Breakdown of Nations,* set the agenda for the small-scale approach. In contrast with the theories of the Old Economics, Kohr's prescription is alarmingly simple:

The real problem of our time is similar to the one besetting a mountain climber in the Himalayas. His heart aches, his lungs fail, his ears hurt, his eyes are blinded, his skin erupts, and yet no heart, lung, ear, eye, or skin specialist can help because there is nothing wrong with any of his organs or his skin. His sole trouble is that he is too high up in the air. He suffers from altitude disease. And the answer is not to call in specialists but bring him down to a lower level. Only if he feels any of his pains still at lower altitude does it make sense to call in a physician.

And so it is with the *social* diseases of our age. It is not poverty that is our problem. It is the *vast spread* of poverty. It is not unemployment but the *dimension* of modern unemployment which is the scandal; not hunger but the terrifying *number* afflicted by it; not depression but its world-encircling magnitude; not war but the atomic *scale* of war. In other words, the real problem of our time is not material but dimensional. It is one of scale, one of proportions, one of size; not a problem of any particular system, ideology, or leadership. And since the size, the scale of social complexity takes its dimension from the society it afflicts, it follows that the only way of coping with it is, in analogy with the altitude disease, to bring the size of the society down to proportions within which man with his limited stature can once again assume control over it.

Kohr typically moves by analogy from the specific to the general — a method that brings a frown to the brow of Old Economists. Unlike them, however, his prescriptions convince through clarity and plain common sense.

In this short book the main focus will be on the thrust of the New Economics so far as work, taken in its widest sense, is concerned. In the 1980s unemployment has become, again, a central issue for economic debate and the New Economics has a number of distinctive approaches to the problem. These can be best summarized in the form of alternatives to the three-pronged policies that successive governments have brought to bear. The first, and most important policy that all governments, whatever their colour, declare is what might be termed 'good housekeeping'. There are arguments about the extent to which it is wise to invest and spend taxes to promote growth and demand and, therefore, jobs. But all governments agree that spending levels should not be so high as to increase inflation beyond acceptable levels — acceptability varying from government to government but in the recent past running somewhere between 4 and 10 per cent.

The New Economics does not challenge these propositions. Of course, demand can be stimulated by extra spending and, of course, a judgement should be made as to how far this is possible without causing inflation to rise too high. But the question is, does government tinkering with the economy along these lines make a great deal of difference? Instead, the New Economics emphasizes the importance of the local economy, a concept explored in detail in the next chapter, and argues that this is where the main impact is made so far as jobs are concerned. The Old Economics regards the local community and economy as simply a scaled down version of the national picture; the New Economics views it as having a clear identity of its own with the need for it to take definite steps to look after its own future. As one enthusiastic exponent of the local economy, Guy Dauncey, has put it:

> Two thousand local towns and cities can each generate 1,000 jobs (or remove 1,000 people from the dole queue) with more ease than central government can generate two million jobs (or remove two million people from the dole queue). It is local effort, local planning and local initiative that will make the difference over the next decade.

The second broad government policy for tackling unemployment is to promote small businesses, with varying degrees of urgency, using a combination of loan guarantees, tax incentives and start-up grants. The alternative New Economic approach is, again, not to oppose the policy as such but to question its relevance for many run-down areas of the country where there are simply very few entrepreneurs in the traditional sense to be found. Instead, a new blend of entrepreneur has to be nurtured — people less concerned with getting rich or with the profit motive as such, and more concerned with keeping the community alive, often in an area where the economy may have virtually ceased to exist. For the New Economics this kind of entrepreneur is most likely to be found as part of a worker co-operative and there are encouraging signs that these are rapidly increasing, especially in areas badly hit by unemployment. The flowering of a new wave of worker co-operatives in the 1980s is explored in chapter 3.

The third policy approach of successive governments for coping with unemployment is to spend large sums — in 1985 some £2 billion — on a variety of palliative Youth Training and Community programmes. These are geared to removing as many people as possible from the unemployment statistics and as operated are palliative because they do not constitute a fundamental attack on the problem. The approach of the New Economics here is to say that these resources should be used more imaginatively to create permanent jobs, especially in the environmental field as discussed in chapter 4, rather than merely removing people from the dole queue for one or perhaps two years.

A classic example of the New Economics working on the ground in this area is the Cyclepath Project which has already made a major environmental and job creation impact and has potential for even more. The director of the Project, John Grimshaw, has surveyed more than 3,000 miles of disused rail tracks and canal towpaths which are suitable for conversion into 6-ft wide cyclepaths. So far 700 miles have been constructed with the longest a 35-mile route starting in Avonmouth and passing through the Bristol connurbation to Bath. Much of this work has been done in conjunction with local authorities and using Manpower Service Commission job-creation scheme money. But if a proper full-scale programme was launched some 10,000 jobs could be created compared with just 3,000 currently working on projects in various parts of the country. The cost-benefit equation in extending the scheme as part of a more integrated transport policy and as a highly effective method of job-creation is easily made. As John Grimshaw says:

> Over the last 30 years transport funds have gone almost exclusively into new roads for heavier and faster vehicles and both cyclists and pedestrians have had a very bad deal as a result. Our cities have become more polluted and the number of accidents to cyclists have increased. A national cyclepath network would boost the amenity and tourist value of our cities, meet a growing demand from cyclists, and create a great deal of work in the process.

In its combination of creating socially useful work and enhancing the environment the Cyclepath Project exemplifies perfectly the message of the New Economics. How this holistic philosophy can be applied throughout the economy and its implications for the future of work are the main themes of this book.

● John Grimshaw, director of the Cyclepath Project. In its combination of creating socially useful work and enhancing the environment, the Project exemplifies perfectly the message of the New Economics.

The Ecological Imperative

Underlying the New Economics is a deep awareness that any prescriptions for the future must take into account their impact on the environment. The point has been most graphically driven home by the American economist and futurist Hazel Henderson:

> I like to think of the total productive society as a three-layered cake with icing on the top. The icing is the private sector — what most

economists think is the most important layer because they actually believe that this is where all wealth is created.

The next layer down is the public sector containing the whole infrastructure of society — the health and education services, supply of gas and electricity, the construction of roads and so on. Most conventional economists have by now come to admit that

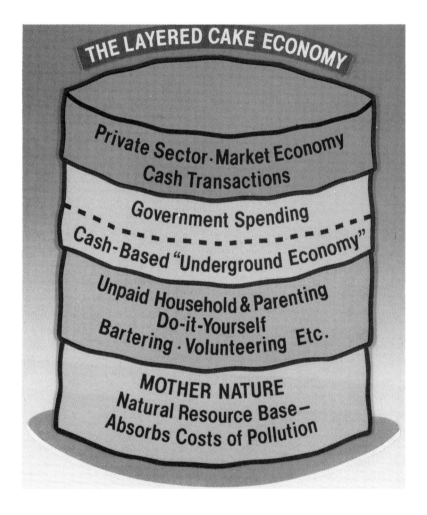

THE LAYERED CAKE ECONOMY

Private Sector · Market Economy
Cash Transactions

Government Spending

Cash-Based "Underground Economy"

Unpaid Household & Parenting
Do-it-Yourself
Bartering · Volunteering Etc.

MOTHER NATURE
Natural Resource Base—
Absorbs Costs of Pollution

● Hazel Henderson's layered-cake economy. Conventional economists only measure the top two layers. But in reality these are subsidized by the bottom two.

we cannot have a private sector without a public sector, though they still cling to the belief that it is the private sector that subsidises the public sector rather than the other way around.

But these are still just the top two layers of the cake, the only two parts that the old economists measure. Below are two more layers. The first I call the love economy — the social economy of co-operation, household work and parenting, community work and so on. And then, of course, below that is Mother Nature, the bottom layer on which the whole structure rests and which subsidises the whole thing.

The main reason why the macro-economic policies of the Old Economics are failing so badly is because they only take into account the top two layers of the cake. We have been continually forcing the social and environmental costs of the private and public sectors on the bottom two layers of the cake and so it is inevitable that eventually the whole system will break down. What we have to realise is that it is the co-operative economy of the household and the local community that subsidises the gross national product, rather than the other way around. In the same way it is Mother Nature that subsidises the whole cake — just so long, that is, that she can stand the waste and the pollution.

Henderson points to a law of diminishing returns affecting industrial expansion, with Western societies hitting an 'inexorable energy crunch' coupled with bureaucratic bottlenecks brought about by large-scale production methods. When, under these pressures, industrial economies reach a certain limit of centralized capital-intensive production, they *have to shift direction,* to more decentralized economic activities and political frameworks:

This change of direction is a scenario for 'spontaneous devolution', where citizens begin simply recalling the power they once delegated to politicians, administrators and bureaucrats, and the power they delegated to business leaders to make far-reaching technological decisions. The growth in all mature industrial countries of citizen movements for consumer and environmental protection, corporate and government accountability, human rights and social justice; the drive for worker self-management; the growth of the human potential movement, self-help care; 'small is beautiful' technologies; alternative lifestyles; and the rise of ethnic pride and indigenous peoples, as well as the tax revolt, are all parts of this 'spontaneous devolution' of old, unsustainable structures.

The same ecological perspective is articulated by the English economist and futurist James Robertson. He defines the choice

● Futurist Hazel Henderson — there is a 'spontaneous devolution' under way in the old, unsustainable structures.

● James Robertson, speaking at a Press conference during the 1985 Other Economic Summit: 'Instead of a widening split between those who work and those who live lives of leisure, there will be a merging of work and leisure in many people's lives . . .'

Alongside Robertson is Paul Ekins (right), convenor of The Other Economic Summit.

of futures between what he calls the HE and SHE alternatives.
The HE — hyper-expansionist — future holds that:

> . . . we can break out of our problems by accelerating the super-
> industrial drives in Western Society, in particular by making more
> effective use of science and technology. Space colonisation, nuclear
> power, computing and genetic engineering can enable us to
> overcome the limits of geography, energy, intelligence and biology.
> This view appeals to optimistic, energetic, ambitious, competitive
> people for whom economic and technical achievement is more
> significant than personal and social growth. They are often male.
> Their preferred future offers bigger toys and more important jobs
> for the boys.

On the other hand, the SHE alternative — sane, humane,
ecological — holds that, instead of accelerating, we should change
direction:

> The key to the future is not continuing expansion, but balance
> — balance within ourselves, balance between ourselves and other
> people, balance between people and nature. This is not a recipe
> for no-growth. But the crucial new frontiers for growth now are
> social and psychological, not technical and economic. The only
> realistic course is to give top priority to learning to live supportively
> with one another on our small and crowded planet. This will
> involve decentralisation, not further centralisation.

The ecological imperative has highly significant repercussions
so far as the future of work is concerned:

> The possibility cannot now be ignored that employment may be
> becoming an uneconomic way of getting much important work
> done, just as slavery became uneconomic in its time. The realistic
> and responsible expectation must now be, not only that many
> years of high unemployment lie ahead, but that full employment
> may never return again.

The answer, Robertson maintains, is to change towards a more
ecologically orientated society in which increasing numbers of
people organize useful and rewarding activity for themselves:

> Instead of a widening split between those who work and those
> who live lives of leisure, there will be a merging of work and leisure
> in many people's lives. Instead of a shift to a super-service society

dominated by experts, there will be a shift to a self service and mutual aid society; increasing numbers of people will take more control of their work and other aspects of their lives.

Both Hazel Henderson and James Robertson were key contributors to *The Other Economic Summit,* organized in London annually during the mid-1980s to coincide with the 'conventional' economic summits of the Heads of State of the major Western industrial countries. The organizers of The Other Economic Summit identified nine problems for the Old Economics:

- Orthodox policies, whether of deflation or reflation, fail to create sustainable patterns of employment or a sustainable economic base for the future.
- Increases in economic output no longer create corresponding increases in employment. The additional revenue generated by growth is often used by firms for capital investment, which raises productivity at a higher rate than the economic expansion itself, thereby causing unemployment.
- Measures of growth in the economy as a whole mask the fundamental differences between economic sectors; more and more, increases in consumption are now taking place in sectors which can grow without creating significantly more jobs. Moreover, many of the jobs which growth does create are negative in terms of personal fulfilment, social usefulness and environmental impact.
- The objective of 'full-time jobs for all' in the formal economy is therefore no longer feasible. Different forms of work and working will need to be developed to enable people to contribute to society.
- This being so, the labour market is increasingly becoming an unjust, inefficient and inappropriate way, not only of organizing work, but also of distributing income.
- The international banking system, now under great pressure, has enabled the countries of the North to become ever richer at the expense of the South. Conventional patterns of international trade, dominated by multinational corporations, hinder sustainable development in the South. Further increases in levels of consumption in the industrialized world can only exacerbate these problems.
- Even present levels of consumption in the North cannot be

maintained except by excessive depletion of natural resources and massive destruction of the life-sustaining capability of the biosphere.

- In particular, investment in weapons industries is a drain on, rather than a boost to, the economies of arms-producing countries. Such investment not only fuels the arms race, as arms-producing countries seek exports, but also absorbs resources essential for more productive development.
- Thus the personal, social, environmental and spiritual costs of pursuing indefinite industrial expansion (as measured by increases in GNP) already outweigh the material advantages of such a policy. Yet conventional economics, whether of Right, Left or Centre, seems incapable of identifying or evaluating these costs. It has become an instrument of impoverishment, blindly promoting ever-greater exploitation of people, resources and the environment, in ways that work against the interests of the vast majority of people.

The report of the first Other Economic Summit, held in June 1984, concluded that the theoretical basis for 'contemporary economic policy' — that is, the Old Economics — had become invalid. The purpose of the Other Economic Summits was to bring together people engaged in working out alternatives:

> The New Economics will never be handed down from above on tablets of stone. Rather it will emerge, as more and more people subscribe to the personal, social and ecological awareness in which it is rooted, and start to live and work accordingly . . . It is an evolutionary, progressive cycle, fuelled by the new values and attitudes of the post-industrial age.

The Third Sector

At the opening of his book *Good Work,* Schumacher identified three purposes of human work: to produce necessary and useful goods and services; to enable us to use and perfect our gifts and skills; and to serve, and collaborate with, other people, so as to 'liberate ourselves from our inborn egocentricity'. Looked at in this way it can be seen at once how narrow is a definition of work that sees it just in terms of paid employment. Indeed, as will be argued in the final chapter, even those in a conventional paid job can, in future, expect to be spending less and less time doing it. In his *The Future of Work* Charles Handy, of the London Business

School, predicts that the 100,000 hour job — 47 hours a week, for 47 weeks a year for 47 years — is already crumbling (down to 75,000 hours in many offices where a 35 hour week is the norm) and that the 50,000 hour job will become commonplace by the early 1990s. As he says, this will mean for the majority of people shorter working weeks, shorter working years, and shorter working lives in the conventional sense of working. However, this does not mean that there will be more conventionally paid work to go round as a result. Nor does it mean that people will want to work less, in the sense of work as defined by Schumacher.

A survey in the *Guardian* newspaper in December 1981 asked what were the main elements in job satisfaction. Top of the list came personal freedom, respect of colleagues, learning something new, challenge, completing a project, helping other people. Twenty-fourth on the list was money; seventeenth was security. One may question the precise order of these priorities but what they, nevertheless, indicate is that a job, at least ideally, is seen primarily as a means of fulfilling oneself and relating to other people. In future everybody, not just those who are unemployed in the sense of being without paid work, are going to have to come to terms with these requirements *outside* work as conventionally defined.

Because of this the New Economics regards the mass unemployment that society is presently experiencing as containing within it an opportunity — an opportunity for changing society's values concerning work; for expanding the concept beyond a mere cash transaction into the holistic vision defined by Schumacher. Nowhere has the potential been better illustrated than by the creation in 1981 of BURN — the British Unemployment Resource Network — based in Birmingham. Essentially it is a forum for exchanging information and offering support to an extraordinary variety of unemployment groups, centres and projects that are continually springing up across the country. The BURN directory, published in 1984, lists more than 1,500 such groups and BURN magazine, published quarterly, provides a continuous update on new initiatives. Among the most important are Unemployment Resource Networks, by now based in most centres of population, which provide a meeting point, advice centre and stimulus for unemployed people to start working on their own terms. The experience has been well described by the Editor of BURN magazine, David Hopson:

For the employed the day, the week, the year, still have a clear structure — time and spare-time still means something, and the latter is highly valued. Their expectations, hopes and plans for the future remain realistic and achievable.

Their status and identity is, if anything, more clearly defined than ever before. People in work are working harder than at any times in their lives (it's a beef I often hear from employed people) and morally they feel even more certain of the value of their social contribution — and the invalidity of ours!

In the light of all this, it is clear why unemployed people as individuals and as a 'class' have come to feel and to be isolated from their families, neighbours, friends, the community and society at large. Our experience and understanding of 'life' has become very different from that of the majority's.

We've got through the first stage of breaking that isolation, however. In drop-in centres and the like we've found a way of making contact with each other. We've found ways of ridding ourselves of much pointless anger and frustration (without blunting our ability to provoke change). We've acquired the skills and experience to help others get through the crap of surviving The New Order. Now we're moving on, and it's time to recognize and define the next stage of our activities.

We're now in the business of finding and developing new occupations for ourselves. We're encouraging and facilitating opportunities for work, and job sharing. We're looking closely at local economic developments for ways to improve work opportunities and use resources more effectively. We're doing things collectively to improve the quality of life — from meeting together, to providing tools-libraries, to backing community arts etc., etc. We're reasserting our value to the community through the things we are able to do for others, and for the environment. We're developing new programmes of education — finding, sorting and spreading information and knowledge which helps us to organize our lives better. We're beginning to establish the idea that unemployed people are not a pool of labour prepared to lie around idly until the system gets thirsty and sucks us in again, which won't happen anyway.

The most important focus for the activities we're engaged in are the communities in which we live. In rural areas, industrial towns, manufacturing centres, and the inner cities, the only level at which we as individuals and small groups can have any real effect, is at the local level. What we're about can be defined, for better or worse, as community development.

As the world of paid employment and the world of those

outside the formal economy, those categorized as unemployed, draws closer together — at least so far as the spare time both have available — the outline of what can be called a Third Sector of the economy begins to emerge. It is in this sector that the New Economics mainly operates, rather than in either the public or private sectors. Paradoxically, however, both the public and private sectors are from time to time drawn into involvement with the Third Sector. For instance, the Manpower Services Commission and its Youth Training and Community Programme schemes are often tapped to boost Third Sector activities. And, as will be seen in the following chapter, many private sector companies have recognized their own self-interest in coming to the aid of the local economy. The Third Sector has achieved recognition at the highest level. For instance, in 1984 a report from the Organisation for Economic Co-operation and Development (OECD) secretariat stated:

> The third sector borrows some of its characteristics from the private sector: autonomy, private initiative, drive for efficiency and competitiveness, decisions based on cost-benefit considerations . . . But its aims are collective in nature and similar to those of the public services.

The Old Economics finds the Third Sector difficult to come to terms with because its cost-benefit considerations take into account the ecological impact of economic activity. There is a further difficulty since, to a large extent, the Third Sector is impossible to measure statistically. This is simply because of the increasing role of the informal economy: the time, energy, and capital devoted to substituting unpaid work for services that once provided conventional employment in the market-place. The best example is household domestic work. A study of the informal economy in 1984 found that each day more than 40 million people in Britain spend from 75 minutes (for employed men) to 372 minutes (for housewives) in domestic work, so that in total 7.5 billion minutes are spent working in the home on an average day. This compares with 7.8 billion minutes spent working in the formal economy by those 23.4 million people still employed. It has been estimated that if domestic work were charged for it would amount to 40 per cent of the value of the formal economy.

Most of the activities described in this book veer closer to the formal than the informal economies. But, as will be argued in the concluding chapter, the two are gradually merging. It is in this context that the New Economics must be considered. During the early 1980s *Work and Society,* a research group drawn from business, trade unions and the Universities published fifteen reports on the future of work. In 1984 a further report appeared, reviewing the previous surveys and summarizing their recommendations. It concluded:

> The fundamental lesson we must consider is that a collapse of paid employment does not automatically mean a collapse of work, and perhaps more importantly need not result in the economic hardship of those unable to gain access to what paid employment remains. There is more than enough work to be done in our society, and even in the depths of recession, sufficient wealth to avoid the extremes of poverty. There must be a gradual uncoupling of work from the means of earning a living.

Source Guide

There is now a burgeoning literature on the New Economics. As suggested in this opening chapter, the best place to start is with the work of E. F. Schumacher and Leopold Kohr. Schumacher's *Small is Beautiful,* was first published in 1973 (now available in paperback, pub. Abacus). Schumacher died in 1977. But the follow-up volume he planned, *Small is Possible,* a survey of his ideas in action, was completed by George McRobie, director of the Intermediate Technology Group (Jonathan Cape, 1981). A companion volume is Schumacher's own *Good Work* (Jonathan Cape, 1979).

Leopold Kohr's seminal work, *The Breakdown of Nations,* was first published in 1957. It is now available in paperback from Christopher Davies Publications Ltd, 4/5 Thomas Road, Swansea, as are his *The Overdeveloped Nations* and *Development Without Aid.* These and many of the books that will be referred to later are available from the Schumacher Book Service, an arm of the Schumacher Society. This operates from Ford House, Hartland, nr Bideford, Devon. Send a stamped addressed envelope to this address and they will return a comprehensive list of the books they have in stock, many connected with the New Economics. Hazel Henderson's book *The Politics of the Solar Age: Alternatives to Economics* (New York, Doubleday/Anchor) is available from the Schumacher Book Service, as is James Robertson's *The Sane Alternative,* published by the author. A comprehensive account of Robertson's thinking is contained in his *Future Work*, published by Maurice Temple Smith in 1985, also available from the Schumacher Book Service.

Charles Handy's *The Future of Work* (Basil Blackwell, 1984) is a cool look into the future with a comprehensive set of recommendations of how we should cope in a world of shrinking paid employment. *The Collapse of Work* by Clive Jenkins and Barrie Sherman (Eyre Methuen, 1979) predicted the growth of unemployment with uncanny prescience.

The Secretary of The Other Economic Summit, Paul Ekins, can be contacted at 42 Warriner Gardens, London SW11 4DU. Send a stamped addressed envelope for a list of conference papers.

The Cyclepath Project can be contacted at 35 King Street, Bristol, or 41 High Street, Wem, Shrewsbury. In 1983 it published *A Guide to Routes in the Making,* a progress report on fourteen routes that were in the process of construction at that time. In 1982 John Grimshaw published a *Study of Disused Railways in England and Wales,* a report carried out for the Department of Transport and available from Her Majesty's Stationery Office. This is a comprehensive account of all aspects of the Cyclepath Project.

The British Unemployment Resource Network (BURN) is based at the Birmingham Settlement, 318 Summer Lane, Birmingham B19 3RL. Its directory, *Action with the Unemployed,* published in 1984, is available from this address. The quarterly BURN magazine has its editorial office at the CRS Offices, 105 Station Road, St Blazey, Cornwall. One of the founders of BURN, Guy Dauncey, has published two comprehensive handbooks for the unemployed: *The Unemployment Handbook* (1981) and *Nice Work if you can get it — How to be positive about unemployment* (1983) available from The National Extension College, 18 Brooklands Avenue, Cambridge, CB2 2HN. Dauncey's perspective is very much that of David Hopson, quoted in the chapter — arguing that the local economy and community initiatives offer the best prospect for most unemployed people. His ideas are further outlined in a paper presented to the 1984 Other Economic Summit: *The New Local Economic Order.*

Church Action with the Unemployed (146 Queen Victoria Street, London EC4) published in 1984 *Action on Unemployment,* an account of 100 projects with unemployed people throughout Britain. An excellent example of the kind of enterprise being started by young unemployed people is Instant Muscle, now an umbrella organization offering advice and support for young people setting up their own small businesses, mainly services such as child care, leaflet distribution, handyman services, gardening and office services, often on a co-operative basis. Launched in 1981 there were seventy enterprises operating under its wing four years later. The national organizer is Peter Raynes, c/o Rank Xerox (UK) Ltd, Bridge House, Oxford Road, Uxbridge, Middlesex, UB8 1HS. The organization's target for 1985 was to help 250 young people establish independent businesses at a cost in training and advisory services of £1,000 for each job created.

Two other organizations helping specifically young people start out in business are: Livewire, based at the National Extension College, 18 Brooklands Avenue, Cambridge — a scheme which offers finance to people aged 16-25 who have an idea for starting a business venture; and Jobstart, based at Old Robinson Building, Norfolk Place, St Johns Street, Bedminster, Bristol, which works with the Manpower Services Commission in encouraging young people to set up on their own. Jobstart is linked with the Bristol Youth Education Service, 14 Frederick Place, Clifton, Bristol, which has a comprehensive list of publications connected with youth training and work.

A self-help initiative for older unemployed people is the Job Change Project, based at the School of Management Studies, Polytechnic of Central London, 35 Marylebone Road, London NW1. It aims to bring together unemployed professionals to sharpen their skills and help them find or create paid employment.

The most comprehensive and up-to-date account of the Informal Economy and its relationship with the Third Sector is the Work and Society report *A Guide to the Informal Economy* (1984) by Graeme Shankland and distributed by the Institute of Manpower Studies, Mantell Building, University of Sussex, Falmer, Brighton. The project has published fifteen reports, summarized by Paul Sparrow in *Working Towards the Future* (1984).

2. Community Initiatives and the Local Economy

> Releasing local energy and initiative is a bit like splitting the atom.
> It is hard to do. But, once it is done, the results are incalculable . . .
> — George McRobie, director of the Intermediate
> Technology Development Group

One of the more outstanding characteristics of rising unemployment in the 1980s is its uneven spread. Britain is a relatively small country geographically. Yet the experiences of people in different regions contrast dramatically. In southern England, particularly the London stockbroker belt and the 'golden corridor' along the M4 motorway, unemployment is virtually non-existent. The outstanding problem for industry in these areas is the shortage of enough people with the skills that are needed.

But travel to other regions — to the West Midlands, the North-East, Liverpool, west-central Scotland, or the valleys of South Wales — and the impression is one of having moved to under-developed countries. In some communities in these areas unemployment is higher than 30 or 40 per cent. Their housing and community facilities are typically run-down, illness prevalent and health provision and social services generally poor. The attendant social problems — crime, vandalism, drug-taking — are depressingly familiar.

In short, the two-class society discussed in chapter 1 — the one with, and the other without, conventional paid employment — has a distinctive spatial dimension to it. Draw a line on a map between the Bristol Channel and the Wash and the class you belong to will be affected by which side of it you inhabit. If you live in south-east Britain the chances are you will belong to the class that has work. If you live in north-west Britain there is a greater chance you will belong to the class without work. By 1986 unemployment was 60 per cent higher north of the line than south. The division is, of course, reflected politically, with the Conservatives dominant in the South-East and Labour in the North-West.

The contrast between the two areas has been heightened by the economic recession of the 1970s and 1980s with its precipitous decline of the traditional extractive and manufacturing industries that were concentrated in north-west Britain — coal-mining, steel-making, shipbuilding, textiles. But the division is older than the current recession. It began as the nineteenth century industrial revolution gathered pace and has accentuated through the present century.

The nature of capitalist economic development is that it does not spread evenly throughout the regions of a country. Experience has testified that within all capitalist countries (and combinations of capitalist countries, like the EEC) economic development ensures that rich regions get progressively richer and poorer ones progressively poorer. Labour and capital tend to be sucked out of the poorer regions into the richer ones. And there is a reverse flow the other way: goods and services from the richer regions flood into the markets of the poorer ones, putting local firms out of business. Leopold Kohr has formulated this process into his 'Law of Peripheral Neglect' which states that concern for remote districts diminishes with the square of the distance from the seat of power. In other words, in large states the regions close to the capital progress, while the distant ones regress, for the same physical reason that is behind the melancholy saying, 'Out of sight, out of mind'.

There are two sides to this coin. The most obvious is the tendency to create a branch-factory-orientated economy in the periphery — and branches, by definition, are vulnerable to recessionary winds. At the same time, the decision-making centres of such economic development must, also by definition, be located at the core and not the periphery. This is the other side of the coin. For where decisions are taken — generally, the metropolitan South-East — economic rewards are highest and people with drive and energy concentrate. For instance, in an electronics company the tendency will be for the best scientific and engineering brains to be drawn near the centre so they may participate in the policy-making process. In turn laboratories and therefore employment prospects also gravitate towards the centre.

The essential antidote to the 'Law of Peripheral Neglect' — and in the context of the EEC the whole of Britain must count as peripheral — is to establish counter-vailing political centres within the periphery. As will be discussed in the final chapter, the devolution of political power to Wales, Scotland and the regions of England is a necessary condition of ensuring decentralization of economic activity. Greater autonomy for Wales, Scotland and the English regions is a central theme of the New Economics. By itself, however, it will not be enough. Devolution and decentralization must go further still, to the localities and communities that make up the nations and regions of Britain. The New Economics declares that local self-reliance is an essential pre-condition of building a sound structure to ensure a working future for the growing class of people who are being denied conventional paid employment.

Circulating Cash
There is, however, very little appreciation of the importance of the local economy in conventional research and thinking. For instance, no university economics department in Britain has a specific lectureship in local economics. One area which would profit from study is the circulation of money so far as it applies to the local economy. The importance of cash circulation is well recognized where macro-economies and controlling inflation is concerned. The impact at the local level is less recognized. A brief look at the experiences of two contrasting communities, Bury St Edmunds in East Anglia and the villages of Newport and Nevern in west Wales should make the point.

During the 1970s a group of local people concerned with the future development of the small town of Bury St Edmunds (population 27,000) formed a Trust. This put forward a scheme to develop a Conservation area in the town that would have re-circulated the proceeds into the community. The plan, commended by the Royal Fine Arts Commission, involved the townspeople raising £300,000 from their own rates (1p in the £ over a six-year period), and borrowing a further £616,000 from organizations such as the Heritage Fund. The development would have taken six years and rents coming in from the newly developed properties would have brought an estimated return on the investment of £156,560 a year — money spent by the townspeople themselves in the new shops and businesses. Over 100 years, it was estimated that £15.6 million would have been available to re-invest in community facilities for the town.

● A home self-sufficient in terms of energy, built by a member of the Newport and Nevern Energy Group. The turf roof provides Scandinavian-style insulation; electricity is supplied by a windmill which keeps batteries inside the house topped up.

The Energy Group have shown that enormous sums of money are unnecessarily siphoned away from communities in expenditure on energy.

The local council never took the proposals seriously. Instead, it invited an outside firm to manage the development. This owned the land and would own the new properties and collect the rents. Its financial projections were that rents worth £322,000 a year would be collected (indirectly, again, from the townspeople themselves). Over 100 years this would amount to £32 million, double the Trust's estimates, leaving the town to enrich people and places elsewhere.

Newport and Nevern are two small villages near the coast in

Pembrokeshire. The population of the whole district is no more than 1,500. In 1980 a small group of a dozen people, conscious of environmental issues, came together to form the Newport and Nevern Energy Group. They began thinking about the impact of high energy costs on the local community not just in terms of the amount individual families were spending but also in terms of the impact on local employment structures and local self-reliance. They calculated that the 560 householders in the district were spending £250,000 a year on energy bills. Even a 20 per cent reduction in demand would produce £50,000 that could be used to benefit the community, money that could be recirculated rather than draining straight out of the area.

So the Group set about encouraging the efficient use of existing energy resources and promoting small-scale power-generating projects such as stream turbine generators, solar panels, windmills and even a water wheel to power an old flour mill. Bulk-purchase of loft insulation material halved the cost and a full-scale scheme was inaugurated with the assistance of the local council, which soon appreciated that its grant aid was achieving more. By 1985 the Group's membership has passed 200 and they reckoned they had more than achieved their aim of reducing the community's total energy bill by 20 per cent.

These two examples illustrate the quite significant sums of money that can be generated, saved and recycled by an imaginative and systematic approach to the concept of the local economy. It really is a matter of common sense. A close examination of the poor and rich areas of any sizable town will disclose that one of the features of the richer areas is that money tends to circulate within them before leaving — through locally-based shopping centres, restaurants, golf clubs. A characteristic of poorer areas is that money spent in them tends to be sucked away without circulating. The American Indian Movement, in its need to build up secure local economies on Indian lands, has declared that locally generated money needs to circulate three times within the local economy by purchasing goods and services from other local people, and thus stimulating further production, before it leaves the local economy in order to purchase an import. The relevance of this objective to our own society has been pointed out by Guy Dauncey, one of a new generation of 'barefoot' economists who have explored the New Economics from the point of view of the unemployed:

The important point is not that every local economy should become a closed system with its own currency and its own protective trade-barriers. That would help nobody. The economic process by which money is leached away from communities, however, through processes of trading and banking, only to be returned in the form of state benefits, is not conducive to the fresh development of these economies.

This simple, but vital, principle is a common theme of an impressive range of local initiatives that have sprung up across Britain during the late-1970s and 1980s, mainly as a response to the recession and unemployment. In 1982 the *New Foundations for Local Initiative Support* published a directory of 98 projects of which only 13 had existed five years previously and the majority, 57, were less than two years old. More have started since then, including the two described below. In his introduction to the directory the editor, Stan Windass, remarked that the emergence of so many grass-roots initiatives aimed at regenerating their own local economies was an indication that 'the economic game was changing':

> People can no longer necessarily expect conventional employment in conventional large-scale industry. There will have to be a resurgence of small-scale economic activity, especially of the kind which reduces energy consumption, capital investment, and transport costs. Maximum use must be made of local resources. Each district must capitalise on what it has and retain, where possible, value-added within the community. At the same time local communities must assume more responsibility for their own health, employment and social policies.
>
> Developments of this kind will not come about alone through top-down planning or government programmes, although government has a duty to facilitate them. They depend in essence on local initiatives. And while so far it has mostly been in the relatively deprived areas that these initiatives have first appeared, they represent a regenerative process of the highest relevance to society as a whole. They are the lifeboats we need as we face the storms ahead.

The Pleck
The Pleck is a small locality of Walsall just north of Birmingham. It has a population of 13,000, about half of whom are of Asian extraction, and an unemployment rate of around 30 per cent. It is an inner-city community which gives the impression of having

been abandoned by the conventional agencies, by local and central government. Dominating the area are six high-rise flats which are the nub of the Pleck's social problems: amongst the people living in them the unemployment rate reached a staggering 81 per cent during 1985. It is a multi-cultural community suffering multi-deprivation: poverty, isolation, racism and violence.

The scale of the problems are compounded by the suddenness with which they came. Even as late as the mid-1970s the Pleck was at the heart of the then prosperous West Midlands. But the recession hit this region probably more cruelly than any other, since there was no experience to fall back on:

> It is despair and rejection that has now washed over the Pleck, washing away even the rage and anguish which was once felt over being thrown on to the scrap heap, and being made to feel a failure. The bewilderment of one day being a vital cog in the production process and surplus to requirement the next, is too much for some people to bear.
>
> The other feeling that prevails is one of the longing, the longing for the old days, when one sweated and toiled and drew pride from one's labour, and satisfaction of 'getting a week in'.
>
> We are fighting against the nihilism of despair. The pulse of our slogan *Changing the Heartbeat of Walsall* is that our children in the multi-storey flats are prisoners in the sky, and so, too, are the young mothers who have to cope with bringing up their children on the subsistence of the D.H.S.S. and in the isolation of 1960s system-built housing.
>
> The view from the balcony of the sixteenth floor is not good for mother or child: one can see the stars, but below is the gutter . . .
>
> But one thing that poverty has not yet destroyed in the Pleck is the will to fight back . . .
>
> We are not claiming to be harder hit than any other former industrial area. What we are trying to do is highlight the positive alternatives . . .

These words are from a fund-raising pamphlet issued by the Pleck Community Association, founded in 1982 as a self-help initiative 'so that we as a multi-cultural community can control our own destiny'. Like most ventures of its kind its existence and success depends largely on the leadership of a few 'larger-than-life' personalities. The Pleck Community Association revolves around the magnetic personality of Brian Bennett, a former local government officer who gave up his job to help launch the organization.

The Association began by harnessing community programme funds from the Manpower Services Commission to set up an Unemployed Day Centre. This provides a meeting place, advice and work experience schemes for the hundreds of people who use it. A sports team organizes football and weight training. A gardening team produces a wide range of vegetables which, together with compressed paper fuel blocks produced by the reclamation team, are supplied free to the elderly in the area. One-and-a-half miles of the canal that runs through the Pleck has been leased, cleared and stocked with fish for anglers.

A church hall has been taken over and used to run a playgroup, aimed especially at the young children and mothers from the high-rise flats. Pleck Community Arts is engaged in painting Walsall's largest wall mural on the sides of the sunken play area in the middle of the ground between the high-rise blocks. In the flats themselves the Association has established common laundry facilities in one empty flat which now acts as a social and advice centre.

But the Association regards the community programme schemes run on the backs of the Manpower Services Commission as only a stepping stone to more permanent ventures. Without the Association and its longer-term objectives they could even be counter-productive, according to Brian Bennett:

> In the economic circumstances we face today, the MSC's community projects are meaningless. They pluck people from the morass of misery they find themselves in, take them on board for twelve months, and then cast them out again. We firmly believe in breaking this circle and our activities in this area has brought us into a certain amount of conflict with the MSC.

One of the first longer-term activities launched by the Association was taking over the local milk-round, followed by the Pleck fish-and-chip van. This is part of a deliberate policy of keeping what little cash the community has at its disposal within the Pleck and circulating it, as Brian Bennett explained:

> The small economic transactions that are carried out within the community, such as general door-step sales of milk, bread, even pop, are quite big business. We find the people who do this are mainly the multi-nationals. We are aiming to replace them as far as possible to keep what money we generate within the community and not have it syphoned off.

● Brian Bennett, charismatic leader of the Pleck Community Association: 'The small economic transactions carried out within the community are quite big business . . .'

The Association has formed a separate company, the Pleck Community Co-operative, an umbrella organization under which a number of small co-operatives are flourishing: a knitwear firm; a building, plumbing and electrical co-operative; and Perfect Car Components which recycles spare parts from old motor vehicles. The Community Co-operative has also taken over the management of a large block of lock-up garages alongside the flats, owned by the council and formerly vandalized, with the result that it generated very little income. Under the co-operative's management the garages have been made secure, are properly tended, and generate an income of more than £5,000 a year.

The money made from these schemes, together with grants from the council and general fund-raising are ploughed back to start new ventures. The most imaginative has been the formation of the Pleck Titans, an American Football team, which has been organized with assistance from America (a coach is on loan from Detroit). Brian Bennett explained the strategy which entailed an outlay of more than £10,000:

> We spotted that American Football is the fastest growing sport in the UK. The American Football league wants to internationalize the game and is making big efforts to ensure that it catches on over here. In that process we reckon there's going to be a growth area in the sportswear and its our objective to make the Pleck the home for the manufacture of this American gear.
>
> But quite apart from that, most of the Titans are unemployed. Now, it's a very boring life being unemployed. American Football

● The Pleck Titans — American football is a glamorous game that offers a break in the boring routine of unemployment and at the same time holds out the hope of creating work.

Note the high-rise flats of the Pleck in the background.

is a glamorous game and offers a break from the trap these people are caught in. I believe they're going to form the basis of professional football teams in the future and that in itself will provide employment.

One of the Pleck Association's major achievements has been persuading the central government to pour urban aid money into the area, mainly for refurbishing run-down buildings especially in the Pleck shopping centre. More than £250,000 was spent on these schemes over a three-year period.

In a very short time in the early 1980s the Pleck Community Association demonstrated the extraordinary talent, flair and imagination that can be unleashed in even the most deprived area. What happened was a self-conscious effort to regenerate the local economy, as Brian Bennett declared:

> Our priority is to alleviate the immediate effects of de-industrialization and unemployment. We have long-since abandoned the notion that government, industry or commerce are going to help us. Our schemes are based on helping people help themselves. Our people have to stand on their own feet because what is the alternative? The alternative is that they will waste away, that the skills they formerly possessed will die, and that the pride they formerly had will disappear.

Antur Tanat Cain

There could not be a greater contrast with the multi-cultural, inner-city high-rise community of the Pleck than the Tanat and Cain valleys close to the English border in north-east Wales. The landscape rolling up westwards from the rich Shropshire farmlands to the rugged Berwyn mountains has a rare individual beauty, special even in Wales. It is a community of small scattered villages interspersed by relatively well-off farmers — well-off because over the last three or four generations they have amalgamated their farms, though in the process hundreds of farm labourers have been thrown out of work.

Unemployment here is not especially high, but only because the area has exported unemployment through emigration. The population has declined by two-thirds in the last 150 years, peaking at about 8,000 in the 1840s and levelling out to around 3,000 today. The most serious loss took place after World War II, with the area losing 30 per cent of its population between 1951 and

1971. Since then the census figures have stabilized, but only because the numbers moving in to the area have equalled those moving out.

Those moving in, to retire or make a living in more congenial surroundings, have disturbed the social structure and balance of the community — though between 50 and 60 per cent of the population still speak Welsh. At the same time it has to be said that much of the energy and initiative that provides hope for the future is coming from the outsiders. A few generations ago the Tanat Valley was one of the richest in Wales for crafts of all kinds. Today it is generally English people who are bringing back spinning, weaving, furniture making, wood turning and engraving, a smithy, and the inevitable clutch of potteries.

The steady haemorrhaging of people out of the Tanat and Cain Valleys has been in direct response to the shift in farming practices. Where once the land supported many labourers who populated the villages, mechanization has now severed the relationship. This is not just a question of jobs. The weeds growing through the rusting market pens in Llanrhaedr-ym-Mochnant, the Tanat Valley's main village, are eloquent witness to the fact that farmers in the valley now go further afield to buy and sell livestock — to Oswestry, Welshpool, and even Shrewsbury. In the process they have abandoned the village stores, though not the village pubs.

The old farming structure was intimately connected with a feudal pattern of ownership and employment in the valleys that persisted until the 1950s. Much of the area was owned until that time by the Wynnstay estate of the Williams Wynn family who still possess Llangedwyn Hall that overlooks the Tanat Valley, a last bastion for the family in north Wales. More than fifty people still worked for the estate in the late-1940s, many of them at the old Llangedwyn sawmill which also included a smithy, shop and pub. But by the early 1950s the complex had fallen into dereliction and this undoubtedly quickened the pace of emigration.

The Tanat and Cain Valleys are a meeting place for boundaries. The area, nine miles wide by about three miles from north to south, edges up against the border with England to the east. But of more immediate consequence is the line between Powys and Clwyd County Councils which at several points cuts the Tanat Valley in half. It actually divides Llanrhaedr-ym-Mochnant in half, the contrasting stonework of the village's hump-backed bridge describing the difference.

It was because the community felt itself on the edge of both

Clwyd and Powys that a group of local people came together to form, first, the Tanat Valley Society, in 1979, which evolved into Antur Tanat Cain (The Tanat Cain Venture) a year later, embracing the neigbouring Cain Valley to the south. By 1982 the venture had won enough support and financial backing to appoint a full-time manager, Dick Richards. With his wife, Gerry, he also runs a restaurant and guest house in Llanrhaedr-ym-Mochnant. Gerry has a part-time job with the Milk Marketing Board, keeping a check on the quality of milk produced by farms in the area. The Richards family — they have two small daughters — are typical of families in the two valleys who derive an income from a variety of sources. Dick Richards explained that it was the lack of a clear identity for the area that impelled the creation of Antur Tanat Cain:

> There was a feeling that we were half a community on the peripheries of both Clwyd and Powys, not to speak of Shropshire. We were crying out for attention from the county capitals but simply not getting it because we were only half their concern and not a strong enough lobby.

Antur Tanat Cain's major project, with grant aid from Clwyd County Council, the Welsh Development Agency, and the Wales Tourist Board, has been to lease and develop the old Llangedwyn Mill site into a complex made up of craft workshops, a museum of rural life, a cafe, giftshop, office and picnic site. When completed towards the end of the 1980s it is reckoned that 60,000 people will visit it during the summer months, giving full-time employment to about sixteen people and a welcome boost to the tourist trade.

Antur Tanat Cain's role goes deeper than creating jobs and promoting tourism. It is about injecting a greater sense of pride, identity and self-reliance into the community. In this endeavour it acts as a supportive agency to such diverse groups as the Tanat Theatre Club, whose sixty members do much to promote the area's solidarity; the Llanrhaedr Playing Field Association, which is raising more than £15,000 in grants to build a sports field for the community; and for the Tanat Cain Craft Guild, which acts as a marketing co-operative for more than a dozen small businesses.

But perhaps its most successful venture has been the *Tanat Chronicle*, a monthly community newspaper produced by an editorial team of volunteers that has appeared with remarkable regularity since 1979. Its circulation of around 1,000 copies, selling for 30p, does a great deal to promote the area's identity. Along with general news, it profiles new enterprises and long-established firms, and acts as an exchange and mart for the community.

● Dancing during Antur Tanat Cain's Mediaeval Fair. Launched in 1985 following the discovery of an ancient charter, this initiative simultaneously promotes community identity, tourism and jobs.

Like most other community initiatives Antur Tanat Cain has made good use of the Manpower Services Commission's Community Programme schemes for employing people for a few years' work experience. One of the more enterprising projects was the employment of a researcher who, among other achievements, unearthed in the National Library of Wales at Aberystwyth, a charter allowing Llanrhaedr-ym-Mochnant to hold two fairs a year. Dated 1284 it is the oldest charter of its kind in Wales and is now commemorated annually with a medieval fair in the village — complete with stalls, archery, a town crier, and a miracle play (performed by the Tanat Theatre Club) that attracts hundreds of people.

About eight miles south-west of Llanrhaedr-ym-Mochnant, along a winding mountainous road, is the most isolated of the Tanat and Cain valley communities, the tiny village of

Llanwddyn. It is separate from the rest of the area, not only geographically, but economically as well. Its most outstanding feature is Lake Vyrnwy, artificially created in 1888 when the first Welsh valley was drowned to provide water for Liverpool. The lake covers 5,000 acres and holds 10,000 gallons of water which can be pumped into England at a rate of 54 million gallons a day.

For nearly 100 years the 300 or so people who inhabit the 'new' village — the old one was drowned beneath the waters of Lake Vyrnwy — have lived in a kind of economic cocoon, with virtually all their work provided by the Vyrnwy Estate run by the water authorities. But suddenly, in 1985, all this was poised to change. The Severn-Trent Water Authority announced that, since it was pulling out of all non-water activities, much of the forestry work of the estate would have to go. By 1990 the sixty jobs being provided would be more than halved to twenty five.

It was a devastating blow and threatened the very life of the village. Could the village post office and stores remain open? Would the village primary school, already facing a falling roll, survive? The villagers responded by calling a public meeting and launching a Community Co-operative to create work. Its vice-chairman is David Rowlands, a native of Llanwddyn and county councillor for the area and who is also chairman of Antur Tanat Cain. He sees what is happening to Llanwddyn as analagous to the experience of many single industry towns in south Wales or the north of England where sudden closures occurred:

> It's the same thing really. This is a one-industry community with one employer who is pulling out. What we have to do is to develop industries which will add as much value as possible, thereby providing as much work as possible, to the indigenous resources we have.

The two indigenous resources that cry out for balanced development in Llanwddyn are, first, the timber grown on the 23,000 acre Vyrnwy Estate and, second, the natural beauty of the area which could be much more effectively exploited for its tourist potential. The Community Co-operative's first success was to raise £8,000 from public authorities in Wales to commission a study by independent consultants on an economic strategy for the area. It also took over the lease on the Vyrnwy Estate sawmill which had been allowed to fall into disuse. And it began thinking how best to promote the lake itself for attracting more tourists.

● David Rowlands, chairman of Antur Tanat Cain — 'What we have to do is to develop industries that will add as much value as possible . . .'

The experience of the Tanat and Cain Valley communities, though peculiarly their own due to their isolation and rural character, are still very similar to what is happening in many other areas of Britain. Faced with a general economic decline and, in some instances, a sudden catastrophic run-down, they have no alternative but to look to themselves and their own local resources for salvation.

The Local Support Network

The Centre for Employment Initiatives, founded in 1982, is a reflection of the growth and importance of community enterprises and the local economy. Based in Liverpool, Glasgow and London, and with a branch office in New York, it is a research and consultancy agency which has mainly aided local authorities in devising new approaches to unemployment and evaluating existing work. By 1985 it had a turnover of more than £1 million and employed fifteen full-time and twenty part-time staff. As a 'not-for-profit' organization it recycles its profits into work for voluntary and community groups on a low or no-cost basis. It publishes a journal, *Initiatives,* which monitors new developments in the local economy field and acts as a forum for discussion on unemployment issues. One of the Centre's directors, Colin Ball, described it as 'a national local initiative'.

Another indication of the growth of the local economy as the basis of the Third Sector described in the opening chapter, is the Local Economic Development Information Service (LEDIS). Based in Glasgow, this produces a monthly publication providing

● Colin Ball, a director of the Centre for Employment Initiatives — 'a national local initiative'.

information on local economic initiatives in the form of case studies. These cover activities such as workspace projects, small business advice and promotion, community businesses, training schemes, new technology projects, enterprise boards and agencies. Each case study is kept to a maximum length of two sides of an A4 sheet and provides details on the objectives, finance, organization and performance of the project being described. During the three years following its inauguration in 1982 LEDIS published more than 150 case studies and developed a subscription list of more than 650 — most subscribers having practical involvement in local economic and employment projects, local authorities, enterprise agencies, central government, and the professions.

The work of both the Centre for Employment Initiatives and LEDIS have revealed a growing network of support for community initiatives at the local level. There are three main agencies that all interact with each other to a greater or lesser extent, depending on local circumstances: local authorities, local enterprise trusts, and local co-operative development agencies.

One clear product of the recession in the late 1970s was that nearly all local authorities across the country entered the field of local economic development which, formerly, the majority had left to central government. Most, by now, have some form of Economic Development Unit which co-ordinates local government's education, housing, planning and financial responsibilities towards the objective of creating jobs. Some have established agencies specifically geared to promoting and assisting community enterprises. Good examples are Strathclyde Regional Council's Strathclyde Community Business Ltd, and the *Community Enterprise Development Agency* set up by the London Borough of Hammersmith and Fulham. Others have set up full-blown enterprise boards, most notably the Greater London Enterprise Board whose work is discussed in chapter 5. Probably the most important input of local authorities in developing the local economy is in mobilizing sources of finance for schemes and enterprises that find their initial inspiration and impetus in the wider community.

And this is where the back-up from the other two agencies is proving crucially important. Together they are providing a framework of practical and expert advice and support which is extremely valuable for small enterprises in the process of getting off the ground. The role and importance of worker co-operatives is fully explored in the following chapter. However, there is no doubt that they would not be expanding at their present rate during the 1980s — around five new ones are being formed each week — without the growing network of local co-operative development agencies. The first one was established in West Glamorgan in 1978. Since then around seventy have been set up, mainly by local authorities. The Greater London Council, together with some of the London boroughs, have funded fourteen Co-operative Development Agencies. An offshoot of the Greater London Enterprise Board is the London Co-operative Enterprise Board, with an investment budget of £1 million. The West Midlands County Council has set up one Co-operative Development Agency for the region and three more for particular areas within it. Welsh local authorities have combined with the Wales TUC to set up the Wales Co-operative Centre which works closely with eleven local co-operative support groups spread throughout Wales.

Alongside these initiatives undertaken by local authorities and trade unions, the private sector has also made a substantial contribution to developing the local economy through its involvement with the Local Enterprise Trust movement. The first one was set up in 1978 at St Helen's in Merseyside by the Pilkington glass-making company when it became clear that a new float glass technology would destroy many of its employees' jobs. The firm set up a trust including representatives from the local authority, the banks and other firms in an effort to create alternative jobs. The initiative proved remarkably successful, though not all the redundancies were offset, and was quickly followed by other areas. By 1981 23 Local Enterprise Trusts were in existence, and their numbers have virtually doubled in each succeeding year — by the end of 1985 more than 250 had been established, probably the optimum level.

The trusts are supported by some 2,500 British companies and at any one time around 250 executives are seconded full-time to act as directors or assistant directors of individual trusts. They offer advice on raising finance, accounts, and tax liabilities. Help is co-ordinated from local authorities on planning matters and making premises available. Links are forged with universities and polytechnics to further research and development. And the results are impressive. During 1984, for instance, Enterprise Trusts assisted the formation of 14,000 new businesses which, in turn, created 35,000 new jobs. The activity is co-ordinated by the organisation

Business in the Community which was set up by a number of large private-sector firms in 1981. Its director, Christopher Norman-Butler, explained their motivation in the following terms:

> It's a combination of altruism and enlightened self-interest. Banks, accountants and solicitors all benefit from the creation of viable new small businesses. The retail trade, manufacturing industry, insurance companies and property companies will benefit from a healthy economy to which the contribution of a strong small business sector is vital. Local authorities will benefit from improved employment prospects in their localities. In fact, all supporters of the Enterprise Agency Movement believe that it is well worthwhile to put some of their resources into helping people help themselves.

The argument, however, goes even deeper than this. The Local Enterprise Trust movement was originally sponsored by the Intermediate Technology Development Group in the 1970s which was anxious to communicate its message in a way that would engage the practical interest and support of local people and organizations. Their director at the time, John Davis, outlined the Group's philosophy as follows:

> Local Enterprise Trusts are more significant than the number of jobs they are helping create — after all, it is firms themselves that increase employment. Their main value is that they are helping communities, which had become largely dependent on others to control their destiny, to take responsibility through local co-operation for their future development and well-being. It is in such an environment that the resource-conserving and environmentally-benign technologies can be introduced widely, and where employment can be found in great variety within the neighbourhood in participative enterprises which operate on a human scale.

Source Guide

There is as yet no comprehensive study of the local economy as the basis of the radical approach to economic planning and organization described in this chapter. There is, of course, plenty of material on regional imbalances and regional policies devised to counter-act them: a good place to start would be the Work and Society sixth report, published in 1982: *Regional Development — Alternatives for the future* by Clara Richardson and distributed by the Institute of Manpower Studies, Mantell

Building, University of Sussex, Falmer, Brighton. But such discussions of regional economic policy still start from a large-scale overview of the economy and take a centralized perspective. Implicit in all the thinking of the New Economics is that we should examine economic problems the other way around. The most sustained effort in this regard has been by Tony Gibson and his work for the Town and Country Planning Association. In 1979 he published *People Power — Community and Work Groups in Action* (Penguin); and in 1984 *Counterweight — The Neighbourhood Option*. This last was a distillation of the experience of more than 100 professionals in the field of how neighbourhoods can control their own environment and shape their own future. Details of this and a comprehensive list of community resource packs can be obtained by writing to: Education For Neighbourhood Change, School of Education, Nottingham University, Nottingham NG7 2RD.

New Foundations for Local Initiative Support is based at The Rookery, Adderbury, Banbury, Oxon., OX17 3NA. It has published three volumes on *Local Initiatives in Great Britain: Vol. I Economic;* Vol. II *Health and Community Care;* and Vol.III *Housing.* They are available separately or as the set of three. In addition it has published *Politics thro' the Looking Glass: the enabling role of government.*

Advice on the kind of activity undertaken by the Newport and Nevern Energy Group can be obtained from Neighbourhood Energy Action, 2-4 Bigg Market, Newcastle-upon-Tyne, NE1 1UW; or The Urban Centre for Appropriate Technology, 101 Philip Street, Bedminster, Bristol. The address of the Pleck Community Co-operative is Mountrath House, Mountrath Street, Walsall, WS1 3NG; and Antur Tanat Cain is at Llangedfan Mill, Llangedfan, nr Oswestry, Powys.

The Centre for Employment Initiatives is based at 140A Gloucester Mansions, Cambridge Circus, London WC2H 8PA. In 1984 it published *Beating Unemployment — a practitioner's handbook.* This is an invaluable guide to the growing variety of initiatives being launched in the context of the local economy across the country. As its introduction remarks:

> Taken individually, each initiative often appears insignificant in the face of a problem of overwhelming statistical and qualitative dimensions. But, when the initatives are assembled together they become more than a sum total of the parts: they show that the

potential to beat unemployment is there, not through 'magic answers' but, more likely, through a coherent and comprehensive set of actions which are part short-term crisis management and part long-term restructuring and investment; part concerned with job creation and part with constructive alternatives to work; part with training and retraining and part with education and leisure; part with the needs of individuals and part with those of the community as a whole; part based on continuation of traditional methods and part with the development of entirely new ones.

The Centre for Employment Initiatives also publishes a bi-monthly journal *Initiatives,* an up-to-date analysis of developments in the local economy in Britain. A year's issues is available on subscription from *Initiatives,* Longman Group Ltd, Subscription Department, Fourth Avenue, Harlow, Essex. For details of the Local Economic Development Information Service, which has more than 650 subscribers, write to: LEDIS, The Planning Exchange, 186 Bath Street, Glasgow, G2 4HG. In 1985 the Centre for Local Economic Strategies was established by a consortium of local authorities with the aim of producing research on the local economy, seminars and conferences, a journal and newsletter. It is based at Heron House, Albert Square, Manchester M2 5HD.

Contacts for local co-operative development agencies can be obtained from the central Co-operative Development Agency at Broadmead House, 21 Panton Street, London SW1 4DR. Business in the Community which co-ordinates local enterprise trusts around the country is based at 227A City Road, London EC1V 1JU. Action Resource Centre, which organizes the secondment of business personel to community enterprises, has offices in most areas of high unemployment, but is based centrally at Henrietta House, 9 Henrietta Place, London W1M 9AG.

3. Working Co-operatively

> In a co-operative we are all the blind workers and we are all the bloody-minded managers, and we have to find a way through because there is no other side to make redundant nor to strike against.
>
> Creating conventional hire and fire jobs is only repeating the pattern that has turned us into a divided nation of employed set against unemployed. But the creation of a thousand commercially viable co-operatives demonstrates that there is an alternative.
>
> — Roger Sawtell, founder member of the
> Co-operative Development Agency

By the mid-1980s the most significant Third Sector alternative to the conventional economy was the new wave of worker co-operatives being established. During 1985 the number of worker co-operatives in Britain passed the thousand threshold and employed some 10,000 people. At the end of the year a further 500 businesses were awaiting registration. What was most remarkable, in the face of the continued economic recession, was their rate of growth. Worker co-operatives were being registered at a rate of four or five a week which meant their numbers were increasing by 20 per cent a year. At this rate, by the early 1990s worker co-operatives will employ more than 25,000 people.

Worker co-operatives, of course, are not a new phenomenon. Their origins can be traced back to the Irish writer William Thomson (1775–1833) who exercised a strong influence on Robert Owen, the nineteenth-century apostle of worker co-operation. By the middle of the last century the emergence of a middle-class Christian socialist movement committed to worker co-operatives prepared the groundwork for the Industrial and Provident Societies Acts of 1852 and 1862 which provided the first legal framework for co-operatives together with limited liability. Another brief boom in the growth of worker co-operatives came soon after World War I when a series of short-lived building co-operatives were founded.

However, there is no historical precedent for the burst of energy and enterprise that has characterized the growth of worker co-operatives in the decade between 1975 and 1985. One undeniable factor has been the economic recession. The large majority of new worker co-operatives are small — employing less than ten people — have a low capital base, and have often been formed by people who were previously unemployed. Of course, there have been economic recessions before, notably during the 1930s. Yet there has never been the same response. So what new factors are at work?

To a great extent the new wave of worker co-operatives in the 1980s have their source in ideals of freedom and egalitarianism that were a characteristic of the generation educated in the 1960s. Indeed, it is this generation that is now most active in forming the new co-operatives, which illustrate in a highly practical way a shift in values. Worker co-operatives represent a breakaway from the hierarchical structures of conventional employment and enjoin a new sense of sharing, commitment, and responsibility. Many of the new worker co-operatives are businesses which have attracted young people who see themselves as part of an alternative culture. Wholefood and health food wholesale and retail enterprises are typical ventures, together with a wide range of craft manufacturing co-operatives.

Another element has been the development of the women's movement in the 1970s and 1980s. It is highly significant that almost half of those employed in the new worker co-operatives are women and, quite apart from any ideological motivation, practical reasons are not hard to discover. In worker co-operatives women can exercise far greater control over their working hours and conditions, incorporate child care needs into their work patterns, and gain experience in types of work not normally accessible to them. By the same token worker co-operatives are an attractive proposition for black workers, hardest hit by mass unemployment, and with little attention paid to their special needs by the dominant culture.

But a third explanation for the new growth in worker co-operatives, and perhaps more fundamental than the two just outlined, is an awareness that the current economic recession is more than just another cyclical downturn. Underway is a technological revolution that threatens to make the very concept of work redundant for large numbers of people on a long-term basis. By their very nature, worker co-operatives are labour intensive and a reaction to the investment imperitives that appear to dictate the decisions of larger-scale private and state industry — whereby more investment, more growth and expansion, inevitably seems to mean fewer jobs. In worker co-operatives the opposite is the case: expansion invariably means more work for people rather than machines. Worker co-operatives are about people taking their own future in their own hands. In the 1970s it may have been at heart a middle-class movement inspired by a combination of the alternative and feminist thinking of the 1960s. But by the 1980s these impulses had evolved through harsh necessity into a much broader movement with working-class people at the cutting edge. For them it was not so much a question of ideology or even ideals, more a straight choice between worker co-operation or unemployment.

Bradbury Street

A good example of this reality can be found at Bradbury Street in Hackney, one of the poorest and most deprived areas of London. The urgency of its problems was expressed during 1985 by a banner across the entrance of the town hall: '20,330 people in Hackney are Out of Work', adding that the figure represented one in five of those eligible to work.

In the early 1980s Bradbury Street, a narrow link between two bigger roads in the heart of Hackney's shopping centre, was derelict. Today it is the home of eighteen co-operatives giving employment to nearly 100 people. It is a bustling place: the shopfronts taken up with co-operatives like Mosquito Bikes, Alpha Omega (TV and Hi-Fi repairs), Buds and Blooms (florist) and Honeybee (furniture restorers), while above them, in two further storeys, are more co-operatives such as Anarres video, Matrix (feminist architects) and Tekke Music which makes African drums.

Kevin Sheridan, one of the members of the Anarres video co-operative, is a native of Hackney and like many other members of co-operatives in the street, was previously unemployed:

> A few years ago, when we were thinking about setting up a co-op we would come past here — our house was just around the corner

● Carnival time in Bradbury Street in Hackney, London — home of eighteen worker co-operatives that have created 100 jobs.

— and the whole place was derelict. We just couldn't find premises to start up and then one day, in frustration really, we said why don't we try and get one of these abandoned shops, do it up and get started.

The borough council had already established a Co-operative Development Agency and in 1982 Kevin and others like him persuaded it to take Bradbury Street in hand. They secured urban aid grants from the Department of the Environment totalling more than £200,000 and within a year the street had been refurbished, the work being appropriately carried out by a number of building co-operatives. The director of Hackney's Co-operative Agency, Malcolm Cumberwatch, believes Bradbury Street is a signpost for similar initiatives elsewhere:

● Malcolm Cumberwatch, director of Hackney's Co-operative Development Agency: 'People have realised that central government is not going to take the initiative in areas like ours . . .'

There's been a change of attitude amongst local councils in the 1980s. People have realised that central government is not going to take the initiative in areas like ours and somehow we've got to do it for ourselves. When we started the council was telling us that unless we had fifty people in a co-operative it wouldn't make any impression on the local economy. But that has changed as well. They realise now that ten co-ops with five people is just as good as one with fifty — better, in fact, since all your eggs aren't in one basket.

Kevin Sheridan commented that what has happened in Bradbury Street is representive of the new wave of co-operatives developing across Britain:

The early worker co-operatives started in the 1970s were rather more idealistic, often set up by people with qualifications — middle-class people really — trying to find new ways to work. But now people are coming to co-operatives because they are desperately trying to find a solution to their unemployment problem.

This judgement is borne out by the flow of people knocking on the door of the Co-operative Development Agency which has offices around the corner from Bradbury Street. Where there was just a trickle of inquiries, now there are four or five groups a day and a questionnaire and appointments system has been instituted.

Also just around the corner from Bradbury Street is another remarkable co-operative initiative, Bootstrap Enterprises, which offers a unique package of assistance to unemployed people seeking to establish worker co-operatives. It was set up in 1980 by Kevin Tunnard who worked during the 1970s for overseas aid agencies in central America. Returning home he realized that many of the needs in under-developed countries were matched by comparable needs in deprived areas of Britain itself:

We try to work with client groups which would not normally think of setting up worker co-operatives. When we set up Bootstrap Enterprises the Co-op movement was missing a whole category of working class unemployed people. So we decided from the start to discriminate against people with formal qualifications who came to us. These we sent off to the conventional support agencies in the belief that they should have enough initiative to get by without the special help we offer.

When they start up all worker co-operatives, and, for that matter, any small business, need three things urgently: workspace, money, and advice. Bootstrap Enterprises quickly realized that, while usually one or even two of these commodities could be relatively easy to put together, it was rare to find them in combination. So they established their building as a workshop nursery, tapped industry and local authorities for small amounts of capital to offer as loans to budding co-operative enterprises, and now have three full-time workers who provide on-site advice, encouragement and support.

Industrial and commercial donors like Barclays Bank and British Petroleum have made small donations to Bootstrap Enterprises which in turn has lent the money. Over the first five years repayments have allowed Bootstrap Enterprises to build up its own independent fund of £30,000.

The money, loaned out in small sums of between £1,000 and £3,000 often for stock to expand a business, is invaluable for co-operatives at the point of start-up when they are often in too weak a position to approach the banks on their own behalf. By 1985 Bootstrap Enterprises had assisted the launch of ten worker co-operatives, each employing around two or three people. They included a cafe, a furniture upholsterer's, a builder's, a motor bike spares and repairs shop, and an optical prescription house servicing opticians. The aim was to move away as far as possible from the type of activity traditionally associated with worker co-operatives until the mid-1980s, namely wholefood shops.

In addition, Bootstrap Enterprises took the novel step of itself researching a market, deciding a co-operative could survive producing for it, and then advertising for people to come and form one. This was the case with Mosquito Bikes in Bradbury Street, a four-man co-operative which repairs and sells bicycles.

Like most of the initiatives explored in this book Bootstrap Enterprises, and Bradbury Street itself, depends on the vision and energy of a few dedicated individuals who have intimate knowledge of their own area. By definition, therefore, such initiatives have to remain local. But this does not mean they cannot be emulated.

Background to the New Wave

Worker co-operatives are businesses owned and controlled by their members, with membership being open to all employees. A strict definition that would embrace all co-operatives is impossible, since the essence of the approach is flexibility and this entails differences in working practices. Nevertheless, it is fair to say that the new wave of co-operatives being created in the 1980s would broadly adhere to the following five principles:

1. Membership is open and voluntary — without artificial restriction or discrimination.
2. Control is democratic — each member has one vote irrespective of capital or labour input.
3. Capital employed is in the form of loan stock or re-investment profits and carries no element of control.
4. Any economic surplus belongs to the members. After providing for reserves for the development of the business, the balance should be distributed to members in an equitable way.
5. Co-operatives are socially and ecologically responsible and seek to work in practical ways with other co-operatives.

Co-operatives begin in three main ways. They may be rescues of ailing capitalist firms. They may be conversions of successful ones. Or, like the overwhelming majority of the new wave of co-operatives, they may be entirely new starts.

The formation of co-operatives as a result of rescue operations is associated with the mid-1970s, stimulated by the Upper Clyde Shipbuilders work-in of 1971 which opened up the real possibility of workers owning and running their own businesses. In 1974 the newly elected Labour Government funded three co-operatives: Meriden Motorcyles, Kirkby Manufacturing and Engineering (KME), and the *Scottish Daily News*. In each case the workers had challenged closure plans and occupied their workplaces.

Forerunners of the new workers' co-operative movement, they had no pool of expertise to help them transform from capitalist to co-operative business methods. Their problems were enormous. Managers had left and funds were short. Shop stewards faced conflicts in their new role as managers and lacked the expertise needed to run the new ventures.

Meridan survived for nine years, making specialist motorcycles and gave employment at its peak to 720 people. KME, with its wider range of products, from radiators to orange squash, saved some 1,000 jobs for three years. The *Scottish Daily News* had a shorter life. When around 1,000 workers fought to save their jobs, their rescue attempt provoked hostility among fellow trade unionists and a mixed reaction from the public. Combined with market forces this produced an early collapse.

All three experiments raised fundamental questions about rescue operations as a method of creating co-operatives. If a capitalist business has failed, what hope is there for a co-operative to rise from the ashes? Do trade unionists have the expertise to lead co-operators out of defensive struggles and into the marketplace?

The conversion of profitable businesses into co-operatives has, naturally enough, proved more successful. However, there have been relatively few examples. Perhaps best known, and certainly the most significant so far as the general development of co-operatives is concerned, is the Scott Bader Commonwealth. Ernest Bader was a Swiss-born businessman who settled in England in 1912, becoming the sole agent for a new product made in his home country, celluloid. By 1951 he was a leading manufacturer of polyester resins and other intermediate chemical products in a model factory at Wollaston in Northamptonshire. In that year he established the Scott Bader Commonwealth as a charitable trust, making over 90 per cent of the shares of the company and 50 per cent of the voting rights to the workers who have, by now, grown to 500 (between the 1950s and 1970s company sales increased twenty-fold). The changeover was not without conflict, however, and it was only in 1963 that the last 10 per cent of the shares and the voting rights that went with them were given up to the workforce.

Apart from demonstrating the potential for converting capitalist enterprises into co-operatives, the most significant contribution of the Scott Bader Commonwealth was its influence in establishing the Industrial Common Ownership Movement (ICOM) in 1971. At that time there were less than a dozen worker co-operatives in Britain. Their rapid growth subsequently owes much to ICOM's early initiative in drawing up a set of model rules for registering a co-operative as a limited liability company. They were simple to understand and embodied a set of co-operative principles which were pure and workable. Some 800 of the 1,000 plus worker co-operatives are ICOM members and have been formed under its rules.

Common Ownership — the ICOM system — is a form of worker co-operation which limits individual shareholding to a token £1, restricts membership of a co-operative enterprise to those who work in it, and ensures that capital is collectively owned and cannot be distributed to members on dissolution. Although most worker co-operatives in Britain are registered using these ICOM model rules, worker co-operatives and common ownership are not synonymous. The main alternative, associated with Job Ownership Ltd, another organization which promotes worker co-operatives, favours ownership arrangements which combine individual shareholdings by worker owners with a substantial element of collective ownership. This perspective stresses the danger for a collectivist co-operative in relying too heavily on the altruism of the individual members. For instance, since they cannot get at the capital when they leave the co-operative or when they reach retiring age, why should members bother to nurture it? On the other hand, proponents of the ICOM collectivist approach argue that to stress the different financial interests of different members (through their shareholdings) is to introduce into the co-operative capitalist attitudes which are all too likely to destroy it in the end. Perhaps the way to resolve this argument is for a balance to be struck, as the director of Job Ownership Ltd, Robert Oakeshott, has put it:

> There must be substantial individual 'ownership' — otherwise the interests of individual worker-members will not be securely linked to those of the co-op. Moreover, this individual 'ownership' must, at the outset, be purchased, not acquired as a gift, otherwise there will be no psychological feeling of responsible ownership (otherwise, too, the open-door policy of job expansion will be undermined). Yet, on the other hand, there must be substantial and fully protected collective ownership. For, if not, the ability of the co-op to survive and progress will be severely weakened.

Nevertheless, the fact that such a large majority of worker co-operatives in Britain are registered under ICOM's collectivist rules carries in itself a very strong message. And this is that the question of capital is not the central focus for most co-operatives — because, very simply, there is not very much capital around to invest. Rather, the people creating the new wave of co-operatives are investing themselves, often to the extent of going without pay for many months to get their enterprise off the ground.

An analysis of the growth of worker co-operatives between 1982 and 1984 shows the biggest increase in those classified as providing services, ranging from waste recycling through motor vehicle repairs, printing and publishing to record, film and music making. These numbered 562 in 1984, a staggering 124 per cent increase over the 251 that existed two years earlier.

The next largest sector was the wholesale and retail trade, including catering and food processing. In 1984 there were 221 worker co-operatives in this area, a 46 per cent increase over the figure of 151 in 1982.

In contrast, the growth of the remaining major sector — manufacturing — was relatively small: a reflection, however, of the picture in the economy as a whole. There were 128 in this category in 1984, only 13 per cent more than the 113 that existed in 1982.

Despite the lack of growth of manufacturing co-opertives, it is here that the biggest challenge faces the worker co-operative movement. For unemployment during the recession of the 1980s has hit hardest among manual workers and is likely to continue doing so. There is likely to be continued demand too, for women's co-operatives as more and more women come on to the labour market seeking flexible working conditions that fit in with family life — and women's co-operatives are classically in the manufacturing fields of clothing, publishing and printing.

At the same time, and in the opposite corner of the employment spectrum, more and more professional enterprises such as architecture, management, media, computer software, and even legal firms are being registered as co-operatives rather than, say, partnerships.

The following short profiles of three worker co-operatives, all set up in the early 1980s, illustrate the variety, the motivation, problems and successes of the new wave.

Treeworks

The Treeworks woodland co-operative, based at Backwell just outside Bristol, had its origins in the Dutch Elm disease crisis of the late 1970s. The two founders — Neville Fay who had run a hostel in Bristol for ex-offenders, and John Emery, who was attempting to make a toy-making business a going concern — were both partially unemployed and together began to find work clearing diseased Elms. Soon they were joined by another friend, Ben Collier, a former student who had been travelling abroad, and they realized there was great potential in establishing a comprehensive woodland management enterprise.

Deciduous woodland has declined catastrophically over the

● The Treeworks co-operative — Neville Fay (left), John Emery, and Ben Collier who remarked: 'We've supported each other financially and emotionally through many hard times . . .'

last 100 years and what remains is coming to fruition all at once over the next ten years. Almost too late, awareness is growing of the benefits to be gained from properly managing and re-stocking what woodland remains. Treeworks have developed to the point where they can now prepare and carry out a renovation programme for a piece of neglected woodland to make it pay its way. In the process different members of the co-operative have specialized in silviculture (the economics of tree management), tree surgery, and the processing and merchandizing of felled timber.

None of the co-operative members had any formal training in their new craft, or any real experience: they learned on the job and developed their skills to match each new step in the venture. Their major problem has been raising finance since they have needed a sizable capital injection to install expensive electric kiln drying equipment and invest in machinery such as chain saws. The novel ways they have found to surmount their money problems are explored in chapter 5. The local council has been helpful in finding them suitable premises for their warehouse and timber yard, in a disused quarry at Backwell.

The three founders of Treeworks did not set out to form a co-operative. It was just that when they had to establish the business on a formal footing a co-operative seemed the most natural solution. The fact that all three were already sharing living accommodation in a housing co-operative was probably instrumental. But they have found distinct advantages in their co-operative framework, as Neville Fay explained:

> Because you're involved in all aspects of the business and in all decision-making through the regular meetings we have, there is an inbuilt flexibility and scope for making changes. Unlike working in a more conventional company there is no way you can be an unwitting victim of whatever changes happen — you have responsibility for the situation you are in and, as a result, are more prepared and better able, I think, to make the best of it.

Treeworks are expanding. During 1985 they took on another full-time co-operative member to deal with the administration and paperwork, a headache for all growing businesses. There was the prospect, too, for taking on as full members some of the dozen or so people who work for the co-operative on a casual basis. When people join the co-operative they plough in, either in a lump sum or over a period, a £2,000 capital stake. As the co-operative grows, however, the members acknowledge there will be strains and tensions, particularly over the distribution of income. As John Emery reflected:

> Until now it has been a personal business which has evolved out of the efforts of three people. But as it grows I think things will have to get more formalised. For instance, until now how much we pay ourselves hasn't been a problem because, with things very tight, we've just paid ourselves on a needs basis and ploughed as much as we can back into the business. I suppose that will have to change.
>
> We have never actually sat down and put a limit on how many people we should have or what our turnover should be. But we're not empire builders. None of us want to take over all the woodland in the country.

The advantages of starting small, and probably of remaining so, were forcibly expressed by Ben Collier:

> It was only gradually that we gained confidence in what we were

doing. We've spent a lot of years not making a profit — in fact, losing money hand over foot while we were learning. We've supported each other financially and emotionally through many hard times. We still make mistakes sometimes but we've come a long way. And because the three of us work closely together there is a lot of opportunity to kick ideas about and find out the best way of doing things.

Happy Hands

Happy Hands was started in 1980 against the background of massive contraction in the steel industry. The six women who set the co-operative up in Port Talbot all had husbands who had been or were about to be made redundant. The measure of their problem is that five years on most of the men were still unemployed. Happy Hands, however, had expanded, had moved into new premises and was employing twenty-three women.

Nevertheless, ensuring the co-operative survived was a hard and continuous struggle with precious little financial reward. All the women had previous experience working in larger factories but in the early 1980s the recession meant there was little of this kind of work to be found. More immediately, because of family

● Happy Hands at work in their sewing factory in Port Talbot — most of the women here have husbands made redundant when steelmaking in the town was scaled down.

commitments, most of them could not work conventional nine-to-five hours. These were the two main factors that drew them to setting up their own business.

They began work in their own homes, making a sample range of their own garments and selling them door-to-door. Then they raised £5,000 from ICOF — Industrial Common Ownership Finance, discussed in chapter 5 — matched it with another £5,000 from their local bank to buy sewing machines and moved into premises. They were now firmly locked into the CMT trade, which is 'cut, make and trim'. Happy Hands makes up garments for other factories, around 500 items a week, usually skirts. It is hard, unrewarding work, since the profit on each garment is usually very small. To complete their first order the women worked six weeks, seven days a week on ten-hour shifts and still lost £500 at the end of it.

They soon learnt to avoid traps like that. But after five years were still only able to pay themselves £35 for a 25-hour week, below the going rate for machinists. Anything above that and they would have to have started paying tax and insurance. To make that leap would have required a wage rate of around £80 a week, far above the amount they could afford, doing just CMT work. As one of the Co-operative's founders, Chris Davies, said:

> We're in one of the worst trades of all — what a machinist gets an hour is pathetic — you get more for being a barmaid. There's a huge profit to be made at the selling end, but nothing for the workers. That's the reason we're going into making our own garments again.
>
> Finding the market is the key problem. It's easy to get a factory together and start producing but at the end of the day, you must be able to sell. That's why we went over to the CMT trade. We did start off with our own garments, but we had months when we couldn't sell them and that's when it started to crumble.

Using their CMT contracts as the basis of their cash flow, Happy Hands were poised in 1985 to start breaking out of the financial circle that entrapped them. They engaged a designer and in March took a stand at the London Olympia Fashion Exhibition to display a new range of clothes. A selling point was that theirs was a completely Welsh product — a Welsh designer, and Welsh wool woven at Llanybydder in Dyfed. They won a few orders and laid down a marker for the future.

What comes across from a visit to Happy Hands, however, is not primarily the business they are in, or even the strain of making ends meet. Rather it is the spirit and camaraderie of the place. Despite the hard work the women have a lot of fun working together and a new dimension for their lives alongside the pressures of home. As Chris Davies described it:

> We're all committed to the place now; it's become part of us. You've got your own key to open up in the morning and in the school holidays we work an early shift, coming in at 7 o'clock so that we can be home by lunchtime. We have even worked 10 o'clock at night until 6 in the morning to get an order out by the following day.
>
> If you're working in a big factory you are basically given a job to do and a target and that's all you do all day. You don't know how many garments there are in the factory, where they're going or how much the firm is getting. But with us, everyone knows how much work there is, how much has got to be put out, what we've got to do and we're all involved. We've got a big board up and we write down every day how much we have done and we know if it's down it means less wages at the end of the week because the bills must be paid. Mind you, that has only ever happened three or four times, but you've got to be aware all the time of what you're doing whereas in a big factory you haven't got that worry.

Soft Solution

Soft Solution is an example of how the co-operative structure is suited to professional high technology business where the accent is on skill sharing and exchange, flexibility, and the advantages that can be gained from a small, intimate concern. A four-man computer software business, based in Bradbury Street, it was set up at the end of 1982. One of the founders, Shaun Fenson, says their style of working and organization points to directions the software industry is likely to take in future:

> What is happening in the computer software industry is a return to the old skilled workers' situation of a few generations ago. Small groups of people are getting together to pool their skills and resources in ways akin to the old printing workers at the turn of the century.
>
> Small, flexible, outfits like ours miss out on the division of labour that necessarily has to happen in bigger companies. We are in a

● The Soft Solution co-operative walking down Hackney's Bradbury Street. Shaun Fenson, on the right, says they are returning to the 'old skilled workers' situation of a few generations ago . . .'

better position to take advantage of expansion and, I think, less likely to run into financial problems because our overheads are smaller.

All four members are in their twenties and formerly worked in larger, more conventional companies, two of them in the video games market. Soft Solution has carved out a niche supplying software packages for steel foundries throughout Britain, an unlikely but growing sector of the business. By 1985 they were paying themselves between £7–8,000 a year, compared with the £10–12,000 they could have expected if they had remained employees in a larger firm. All agreed, however, that they were more than compensated by being in a better position to choose the kind of work they liked doing and by the flexible hours. They work whenever they want — at home or in their small office — with the only proviso that they keep roughly on a par with each other month by month. An additional advantage has been the feeling that they are in charge, running their own company, with the prospect of bigger rewards in future.

Their main problem, in common with most small businesses lifting off the ground, has been developing a market, broadening their client base, and planning a programme of work for more than three months ahead. Quotations have proved a major headache, along with the administrative side of the business. Experience has taught them to keep contracts as simple as possible: wherever possible they limit quotations to fixing an hourly rate for their work (£12 an hour in 1985).

Soft Solution are fortunate in that its members possess skills that are in demand. This has brought with it problems of success. In mid-1985 they were grappling with the need to expand their numbers. What kind of person should they look for? Should they advertise? How would the co-operative cope with taking on additional people?

These issues were thrashed out during one of the co-operative's weekly meetings in April 1985. The decisions reached reveal aspects of both the intimate world of the computer software business and the kind of values that tend to accompany the new wave of worker co-operatives. They decided against advertising, relying instead on contacts to find the right person. However, that decision created problems because they also agreed that they wanted to bring a woman into the co-operative: it was felt they needed a female perspective and contribution and that if they expanded any more before including women members they would be too big and intimidating for this to be accomplished successfully. This condition narrowed the field for potential candidates but it was resolved that they should be prepared to allow more time to find the right, female, person.

Working Despite the System

Treeworks, Happy Hands, and Soft Solution neatly encapsulate much of the experience of the new worker co-operatives of the

1980s. Their message is that setting up a workers' co-operative entails tremendous struggle and often financial sacrifice, especially in the early years. A good deal of self-exploitation is usually entailed. Raising capital is a problem, but more fundamental still is the essential need to have a sound marketing strategy. Most of the co-operatives that have failed have foundered on this rock.

In combining collective action, individual initiative, community concern, and responsible self-management, the new wave of worker co-operatives have transcended conventional political rhetoric. All parties favour them, at least theoretically. Labour has put them at the centre of its jobs strategy for the 1980s, despite reservations about their relationship with the trade unions. It now sees them as part of a modernized re-appraisal of its traditional policies for state control and nationalization. At the same time it stresses that they cannot be viewed in isolation of the need for central planning and greater public control of the main financial institutions. As Tony Benn has put it:

> The true role of the co-ops must be found within a new framework of democratic local and national planning for need and not for profit, with objectives that include the idea of socially useful — and personally satisfying — work.

Worker co-operatives, in some respects at least, also reflect Conservative values, particularly so far as increased employee participation, wider capital ownership, and responsible wage restraint are concerned. In 1984 the then Trade and Industry Minister Norman Lamont, stated:

> Co-operatives bring together the interests of those working in an enterprise with the realities of making that enterprise succeed.

And both Alliance parties have stressed the value of co-operatives in breaking down distinctions between capital and labour and developing a less 'class-ridden' society.

Yet, while local authorities have taken the lead in establishing a supportive framework for the growth of worker co-operatives, there has been very little initiative from central governments, of whatever colour. A discussion of the agencies already at work and what could be done is contained in chapter 5. Meanwhile, the growth of the new wave of worker co-operatives in the 1980s is happening despite the system, not because of it. Though still only relatively small in terms of jobs created, they are among the most practical and hopeful beacons of the New Economics.

Source Guide

There is by now a morass of material on all aspects of worker co-operatives. As good a general introduction as any is *Revolution From Within — Co-operative and Co-operation in British Industry* by Michael Young and Marianne Rigge (Weidenfeld and Nicolson, 1983). This contains a comprehensive contact list for agencies working in the field. Another general introduction is *Co-operatives and Community* by David H. Wright (Bedford Square Press, of the National Council of Social Service, 26 Bedford Square, London WC1).

The Industrial Common Ownership Movement, based at 7/8 The Corn Exchange, Leeds LS1 7BP, has published a comprehensive series of booklets on all aspects of the subject including: *The Workers Co-operative Handbook* (a guide to setting up a co-operative); *Co-op Management and Employment* (how to run a co-operative once it is set up); and *Worker Co-operatives* (the role of local authorities). All these titles and others are available from the Corner House Bookshop, 14 Endell Street, London WC2. In addition ICOM publishes a monthly magazine, *The New Co-operator,* with up-to-date news of developments in the field. A year's subscription is available from ICOM's headquarters.

The Co-operative Development Agency is based at Broadmead House, 21 Panton Street, London SW1Y 4DR. Its directory and resource guide, *The New Co-operatives,* edited by Catherine Luyster, is essential reading; the 1984 edition lists 911 worker co-operatives as well as a useful guide to agencies in the field and a comprehensive bibliography.

Job Ownership Ltd is based at 9 Poland Street, London W1V 3 DG. The Open University has a Co-operative Research Unit, set up in 1978, which has researched all aspects of the movement in Britain and abroad — The Open University, Walton Hall, Milton Keynes MK7 6AA.

For details on Bradbury Street contact the Hackney Co-operative Development Agency, 16 Dalston Lane, London E8 3AZ. Bootstrap Enterprises is based at 18 Ashwun Street, London E8 3DL. Treeworks headquarters is Cheston Combe, Church Town, Backwell, Avon. Happy Hands is based at Llewelyn Quay, Port Talbot Industrial Estate, Port Talbot, West Glamorgan; and Soft Solution at 10A Bradbury Street, London N16.

4. Work from Waste

The Government believes that there should be a new national effort to conserve and reclaim scarce resources — a war on waste involving all sections of the community. We all instinctively feel that there is something wrong in a society which wastes and discards resources on the scale we do today.
— Government Green Paper *War on Waste*, 1974

Since the issue of this challenging statement, a product of the growing ecological awareness of the 1960s, precious little has been achieved. By the mid-1980s only a small proportion of the mountain of waste being produced in Britain was being reclaimed. A report from the House of Commons Trade and Industry Committee, *The Wealth of Waste*, in 1984, set out the stark reality: Britain was losing around £750 million a year because of the waste paper, metals, textiles, plastics, glass and other valuable materials it was failing to recycle.

Over half a ton of debris is dumped into the average household dustbin every year, and the annual pile of domestic rubbish is more than 20 million tons. Another 36 million tons of solid waste comes from commerce and industry. According to studies by the Government's Warren Spring Laboratory at Stevenage, up to 60 per cent consists of reclaimable materials.

In practice, only 15 million tons is recycled, realizing more than £1,800 million: but £1,200 million is derived from the ferrous scrap industry, the most technically developed recycling operation. It takes three times as much energy to convert iron ore into steel as is needed to convert scrap. In 1984 about four million tons of scrap was smelted in Britain and another four million exported. But this still left another two million tons that went unrecovered.

Apart from scrap metal probably the most developed sector

of the recycling industry is in reclaiming spare parts from crashed vehicles. The Motor Vehicle Dismantlers' Association has a thousand members throughout the country who strip down cars and sell the spare parts recovered at usually half price. The size of this business can be gauged from the £700 million insurance companies paid out during 1984 on crashed vehicles.

But the potential is still enormous. For instance, using technology developed by the Warren Spring Laboratory a new company, Tyrolysis Ltd, will be collecting and processing 50,000 tons of scrap tyres a year before the end of the 1980s. The end products will be 20,000 tons of light fuel oil, 17,000 tons of solid char fuel, and 7,000 tons of steel scrap. But when this is fully on stream it will still take up less than half the 170,000 tons of scrap tyres that are estimated to be available every year in Britain. Most of them are just thrown onto landfill sites.

Disposing of rubbish on landfill schemes has been relatively cheap and easy in Britain and generally preferred by most local authorities. By the 1980s, however, this method had already become more expensive than incineration in most urban areas and is destined to become more expensive still as waste is transported to more distant sites. The Trade and Industry Committee report warned that 'by the year 2,000, landfill sites in the UK will be very scarce'.

The arguments for recycling are overwhelming. Half the average dustbin in Britain is filled with waste paper — six million tons a year or 16,000 tons a day. Yet only two million tons, 30 per cent, are recovered and recycled while it is estimated that 70 per cent could be re-used. If this happened, millions of trees would be saved — at present a forest the size of Wales is cut down every year to supply Britain's paper needs.

There is an equally powerful case for recycling glass, but if anything the record on this in Britain is worse than for paper. We recycle about 8 per cent of our glass, compared with more than 40 per cent in the Netherlands and Switzerland, 30 per cent in West Germany and Belgium, and 20 per cent in France and Austria. While Britain has 2,000 Bottle Banks collecting around 100,000 tons of waste glass (known as cullet), West Germany has more than 34,000. The collection, treatment and delivery of cullet requires 78 per cent less energy per ton than using the equivalent raw materials — sand, limestone and soda ash quarried from valuable agricultural land. Despite these uncontrovertible facts, the use of non-returnable bottles has soared in Britain, to more than 1,000 million a year in the 1980s compared with under 300 million in the 1960s.

As technology develops, particularly biotechnology, there is likely to be enormous potential in recycling plastic. We consume around 2,000 million tons a year, of which about half is potentially recoverable. Yet only about 5 per cent is recycled.

The benefits from recycling non-ferrous metals, especially aluminium, are even more marked. Using aluminium scrap saves 90 per cent of the energy required to produce aluminium from bauxite. Yet only about half the potential recoverable aluminium is recycled. Similarly, only about half of the 450,000 tons of waste oil produced in Britain each year is recovered.

The Jobs Impetus

Though the arguments for recycling waste are clear, the will to make it happen is lacking. In its written evidence to the House of Commons Trade and Industry Committee the Government declared:

> The chief economic arguments for reclaiming and recycling waste materials are threefold:
>
> (i)   the general need to use raw materials efficiently and thereby save both on them and on energy costs;
> (ii) for the UK in particular, the lack of adequate indigenous supplies of raw materials for much of manufacturing industry, and the desirability of reducing UK dependence on imports; and
> (iii) the need to minimise the cost of waste collection and disposal to industry and local authorities, and reduce the quantities of waste for final disposal.

What was notably absent from this list was any mention of the enormous potential for creating jobs, especially for young people, in a properly planned and co-ordinated waste recycling programme. If this were appreciated then perhaps the political will for putting such a programme into action, utilizing the full resources of both central and local government, might be generated. As it is, the job creation approach to waste disposal is being left to alternative local initiatives outside the conventional system. Indeed, it can be argued that their example has pushed conventional thinking as far as it has gone in at least putting waste disposal programmes on the political agenda.

The practical approaches to recycling waste and creating work that are being developed in the 1980s have grown out of the alternative technology movement of the 1960s and 1970s. In its early phase the movement was mainly concerned with developing alternative energy systems — wind, wave and solar power — often in the context of promoting rural self-sufficiency. Gradually, from the mid-1970s, the emphasis moved away from isolated rural experiments towards what was called 'community technology', more appropriate for local communities, often in urban areas. The major initiatives have been in energy conservation — especially insulation for buildings and installation of simple flat plate solar collectors for heating; and materials recycling — paper and waste recycling, equipment repair and reconditioning, often in co-operatives. In addition, there have been related initiatives in organic food production and distribution; and new forms of transport, particularly the gradual growth of the cyclepath network across Britain, discussed in chapter 1.

The job-creation potential in these activities has been most graphically illustrated by a handful of experimental waste recycling projects promoted by Friends of the Earth, most notably in Leeds, Birmingham, and Bristol. The biggest, and most successful is Resourcesaver in Bristol which is described below. These schemes have shown that it is possible to envisage the present local authority refuse collection system being replaced by a more sophisticated one in which about half the volume of material presently just thrown away is sorted by each household into categories, such as paper, glass, tins, old clothes and textiles, and sump oil. These would be placed in separate containers (usually heavy duty plastic sacks) distributed free to each household.

Of course, some refuse will always remain as rubbish and have to be collected as such. But the aim would be to have an average of about half of the rubbish produced by each household separated out for recycling. The remaining amount of waste that required collection as refuse would then be sufficiently reduced in volume to permit fortnightly collection. Two-week intervals between refuse collections are already normal in some areas and occur everywhere over Bank Holiday periods. In the intervening week a different team would collect the recycleable materials.

Proposed here is a fundamental reorganization involving both costs and benefits. But refuse collection and disposal in Britain under the present system already costs well over £700m a year. It is estimated that the reorganized system would cost no more, with the added attraction of recycling large volumes of material and creating thousands of jobs in the process.

The scheme is the idea of a group of environmentalists in Taunton, known as the Taunton Think Tank, which in its 1984 report, *Jobs Not Waste*, estimated that more than 25,000 jobs could be created. The present refuse collection workforce would be about halved, because there would be much less refuse to collect. But this reduction would be more than compensated by the numbers of jobs that would be created in the labour-intensive reclamation work.

Briefly outlined in this way, a combination of refuse and reclamation collections might appear impractical, even fanciful. Certainly, when the Taunton Think Tank presented their report to the House of Commons Trade and Industry Committee, little note was taken of it. Nevertheless, the success of the few Friends of the Earth projects around the country, most notably the one in Bristol, have given an indication of what can be done.

● Resourcesaver's office — the administrative centre of a recycling initiative that has generated 110 jobs.

Resourcesaver

In 1980 Bristol City Council discontinued its waste paper street collections as being uneconomic. As a result, the local Friends of the Earth Group set up Resourcesaver Ltd to take over the service. Initially it employed a handful of people, but in just four years and with the support of the Manpower Services Commission it grew rapidly, employing 110 people by 1985. Many had been jobless for long periods. Resourcesaver provided a variety of work experience over a year with a good chance of finding a permanent job at the end.

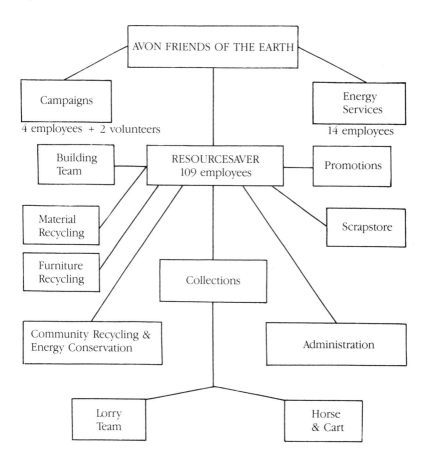

● The operational structure of Bristol's Resourcesaver, Britain's most successful recycling project. It has demonstrated the enormous potential in creating work from waste.

At the start, using a fleet of second-hand lorries, the group concentrated on house to house collections of waste paper. Bristol was divided into areas, with the first task being a publicity drive and leaflet drop in each, persuading people to participate in the monthly collections. Gradually the areas spread to cover most of Bristol and also Bath and the range of materials collected widened to include rags, old car batteries, glass and sump oil. By 1985 sales of these materials was bringing Resourcesaver around £2,000 a month and the group was looking at the possibility of collecting aluminium, plastics and polythene.

At this time, too, Resourcesaver began replacing some of its lorries with horse and carts which have proved an outstanding success. They have brought a great deal of publicity, have proved a hit with the public, and are much more economic to run than lorries. With low cost stabling, the £35 a week food bill per horse is a considerable saving on what would be required to run, tax, and insure a vehicle. As one of Resourcesaver's waggoners explained:

> Horses are ideal for this kind of work. The modern lorry is made for the motorway, not for stop-start duties in an urban street. A horse and cart costs next-to-nothing in maintenance and a horse that shows it can work well in a town gains in value rather than depreciating like a vehicle.
>
> Our method of collection is simple, economical — and easy on the eye. Its better than having a seven-ton lorry crawling around the centre, pouring out diesel fumes in second gear.

During 1984 Resourcesaver achieved a breakthrough when it negotiated a contract with Avon County Council to dispose of its waste paper — an estimated 100 tons a year, worth as much as £40 a ton. Both sides benefited. Avon had been paying £7,930 for a daily lorry collection; Resourcesaver agreed to take it on at nearly half the price, £3,840. Included in the service is the shredding of confidential documents, which has attracted the custom of the Bristol Magistrates Court and a number of offices anxious to ensure confidentiality. Specially labelled fire-proof drums are supplied to offices willing to separate computer printout (the most valuable paper waste) from other office papers. The drums are salvaged from a chemical works.

Each year the volume of material collected increases. During 1984 1,500 tons of waste paper, 100 tons of glass, 1,000 gallons of sump oil, and 150 tons of rags were recovered and recycled.

● Collecting waste paper in Bristol — a horse and cart is 'better than having a seven-ton lorry crawling around, pouring out diesel fumes in second gear . . .'

This success must be as much a tribute to the co-operation of the general public as the enthusiasm of the collectors who, significantly in terms of the concentration of unemployment among the young, are overwhelmingly in the 17 to 25 age range.

Resourcesaver operates out of old factory premises in the Bedminster area of Bristol, which it has converted into different departments. A core team provides the administrative back up, including reception services, typing, personnel, finance and training. There is a building maintenance team; groups engaged in recycling old office furniture and constructing new products such as rabbit hutches, small tables and spice racks out of discarded wood; a canteen staff; and a promotions team to publicize

Resourcesaver's work. During the course of a year people move from one area to another, so gaining in experience and interest. Underlying the whole operation is a common goal of raising public consciousness on environmental issues which gives a sense of purpose, even mission, to the enterprise.

Resoursesaver is, of course, highly dependent on funding from the Manpower Services Commission, but the aim is to hive off gradually different parts of the operation once they are in a position to be self-sufficient. In turn, this creates full-time jobs and frees Resourcesaver to extend its activity in new directions. As Resourcesaver's director, Dick Perry, put it:

● Resourcesaver's director, Dick Perry: 'We regard MSC funding as a seedbed where we can try out ideas, find out what works and what doesn't work and then, when it becomes viable, we hive it off . . .'

If MSC funding was removed tomorrow then Resourcesaver as it exists now would disappear, but there are aspects of the operation that would undoubtedly continue.

What would disappear would be the super-structure. We wouldn't be able to employ a computer operator or a training officer. But our basic activities — the collections, and the furniture and other recycling projects — would continue.

We regard MSC funding as a seed bed where we can try out ideas, find out what works and what doesn't work and then, when it becomes viable, we hive it off.

The first venture to be hived-off was Energy Services, a loft-insulation company that, though working out of the same premises as Resourcesaver is fully independent. It began as just a loft insulation business but now covers the whole range, starting with a free heat-loss survey for a house and then carrying out its recommendations to order. By 1985 it was employing twelve people full-time and arranging £6,000 worth of energy-saving investment a month, including secondary glazing, heating controls and cavity wall insulation (using a waste paper-based product) as well as loft insulation itself. Energy Services has demonstrated that any urban community with a 100,000-plus population could support a comparable business.

During 1985 the first part of Resourcesaver's collecting operation was hived off: one lorry and four workers split away to form their own autonomous operation, aiming at collecting 60 tons of waste paper a month and generating an income of £24,000 in the first year.

A major market for waste paper is, of course, in the manufacture of new paper, using the recycled fibre. In order to stimulate the demand for recycled paper Resourcesaver launched another separate company, Treesaver Paper Products, in 1983. Within two years its workforce had risen to four and it had achieved an annual turnover of £75,000. Treesaver's director Richard Walker, who is also chairman of Resourcesaver's steering group, commented:

Quite apart from promoting demand for recycled paper we are demonstrating that business and ecology can mix — to be in business you don't have to be polluting almost by definition. You can be in business and be environmentally sound as well.

Three ranges of paper are sold: papers for art use in schools and colleges; hygiene products; and a variety of stationery —

● The Scrapstore — an Aladdin's cave of discarded industrial and commercial wastes transformed into materials for children's play.

copying, printing and duplicating papers as well as envelopes. Customers are usually small businesses, other paper merchants, schools, colleges, and shops.

Another Resourcesaver offshoot is the children's Scrapstore, an Aladdin's cave of discarded industrial and commercial wastes transformed into materials for play. Paper, packaging, wood, buttons, tape, paint, everything from empty tobacco tins to scenery is scrounged for sale (at rockbottom prices) to more than 500 playgroups and over 30,000 children in the Bristol area. The store collects well over 160 tons of waste and surplus material a year. In addition, and in collaboration with other Scrapstores around the country, it bulk buys play materials like chalk, glue, powder paint, scissors and paint brushes. The network of Scrapstores around the country now serve more than 7,000 playgroups reaching around half-a-million children.

Resourcesaver in Bristol, and a number of similar initiatives elsewhere in the country, notably Teeside Wastechasers in Middlesborough, are demonstrating in a practical way what can be achieved when environmental concern is linked to job creation.

They have shown that throughout Britain's urban communities there is enormous potential for tapping energy and enthusiasm to create work and, at the same time, protect the environment. What they have achieved, though with the support of the Manpower Services Commission, has been largely on a voluntary basis. If their example was taken up by central and local government in a planned, co-ordinated, programme the potential would be very great indeed.

The Wealth in Waste

While about half Britain's domestic waste could be collected and recycled if the refuse collection system were remodelled on the lines suggested above, this would still leave a large volume of both domestic and commercial material to be processed. New techniques are being developed, however, which if deployed could make profitable use of virtually all the rubbish we produce.

Burning waste to provide electricity and steam for district heating and industrial processes is already being undertaken on more than an experimental scale. One ton of waste contains enough energy to power a generator producing 500 kilowatt-hours of electricity.

Experience in Britain rests mainly on an incinerator at Edmonton, north London, which burns over half-a-million tons a year — about 10 per cent of the capital's garbage. More than £4 million a year is earned, selling power to the Eastern Electricity Board. The cost of running the plant (at 1985 prices) is £18 per ton of waste. Set against that the income from the sales of electricity, then the cost of waste disposal is just £8 per ton, the cheapest of the methods available to the London local authorities.

Edmonton was the first local authority scheme in Britain. Others are following. At Nottingham more than 180,000 tons are being burnt, giving heating to 4,270 homes, shops, offices and hotels. A similar development is being undertaken in Sheffield.

Burning waste in an incinerator has the advantage that very little pre-treatment is needed. But the material can be pulverized and converted into fuel blocks mixed with coal dust. A third way is to extract the most combustible items which are then formed into dense pellets with 60 per cent of the heat energy of coal by weight. There are ten plants in Britain exploiting one or other of these waste-to-energy conversion schemes. The potential is for more than a hundred. In Germany and France well over half their refuse is being disposed of by energy recovery systems. In

Britain only 15 per cent of household refuse is treated in any way, and less than 5 per cent is used for energy recovery. It is estimated that if we had 100 instead of just ten waste-to-energy plants the yield would be more than the equivalent of four million tons of oil a year.

New techniques in biotechnology are making recycling rubbish increasingly economic. The introduction of bacteria and microbes into landfill sites can speed up the commercial production of methane gas. The first British full-scale gas extraction and transmission system was commissioned at the GLC's Aveley Landfill site in Essex in 1983. It provides five million therms of methane gas a year to a nearby factory that uses it to power a steam boiler plant.

Even more innovatory is a waste digestion and recycling process that produces fuel briquettes, building board material and a horticultural growing medium from a combination of domestic refuse and sewerage sludge. The process begins by loading normal domestic rubbish into a pulverizer. Cans, glass and plastic are separated out and the residue is mixed with raw sewage. Anaerobic digestion funnels off methane gas and other processes kill off harmful bacteria.

The operation is entirely energy self-sufficient, using the gas produced by the fermentation of the waste. The two basic products are a papier mâché fibre material which can be used in the board industry, and high-grade garden compost. When the fibre is mixed with coal dust the result is a fuel suitable for both domestic and industrial use.

Developed by WMC Resource Recovery at an experimental site at Avonmouth, near Bristol, the first commercial undertaking went into operation in London during 1986 with a throughput of 360 tons of domestic waste a day.

It is possible to recover an even more valuable product from ordinary domestic rubbish — oil. In 1985, after a five-year research programme, scientists at Salford University devised a process for converting rubbish into oil which, if fully exploited commercially, could meet 10 per cent of Britain's needs. The scientists reckoned their process could average two-and-a-half barrels (100 gallons) of crude oil out of a ton of selected rubbish. Their machine, which simulates in ten minutes what takes nature around 150 million years, costs the equivalent of 20 gallons of oil for every 100 produced — cheaper than extracting oil from the North Sea.

The products that can be made from waste are a hidden

resource in the economy. About half the contents of the average dustbin can be reclaimed and recycled directly, mainly paper, glass and aluminium cans. The residue can be dealt with in the variety of ways outlined above. If properly exploited there is virtually unlimited potential in the wealth and work that can be created out of the material we have grown up to regard as useless and troublesome rubbish.

The Farming Waste Scandal

After the mountain of rubbish we throw away each year without a second's thought to the value and job potential possible with recycling, the greatest waste scandal in Britain is in farming. The issues here are not so immediately obvious and the arguments rather more complex. But, if anything, the question, so far as the environment is concerned, is even more profound than with the disposal of more conventionally understood waste, the refuse in our rubbish bins. The most fundamental resource we have is land and the food we produce from it.

The waste being produced by the bulk of British, and indeed European, farming comes in two categories, one which we could well do without and the other which we are failing to deploy to its full measure. The first is over-production of crops — by around 20 per cent; the second is farm slurry, the natural basis of organic farming.

A good deal of the blame for over-production must be attached to the European Community Common Agricultural Policy and its price support system, which totally distorts the market for produce and positively encourages over-production. But agri-business — farming which smothers the land in machines, chemical fertilizers and pesticides in the name of maximum output per acre of usually single crops — has developed over a much longer period than Britain has been inside the EEC. The result has been an environmental and employment disaster.

Just one area of farming should suffice to illustrate the point: cereal production. During the 1980s EEC member countries have been massively over-producing grain, largely because of the Common Market guaranteed price system, which is 40 per cent above world market levels. Farmers are getting around £50 subsidy for each ton of grain they produce, costing the EEC some £800 million a year. Ironically, the artificially high price has made the product too expensive for the traditional customer, the animal feed compounder. So the mills supplying livestock producers have turned to Third World countries for cheaper substitutes like manioc and maize gluten, yielding a higher profit for themselves but adding to the over-production problem.

In 1985 the EEC's cereal mountain was 14 million tons and projected to rise to 89 million by 1990. Already in 1985 it was costing £200 million a year to store and was even too expensive to give away for famine relief. The 1.4 million tons of grain sent by the EEC to Africa during 1985 was bought on the world spot market: the European commission could not afford to buy back the more expensive grain from the EEC's own stores. In desperation one solution being considered was to turn the surplus into its chemical constituents, notably starch and cellulose, from which plastics and fibre could be made.

The dilemmas of over-production are only half the problem, however. The other is the environmental and employment price that has been paid in achieving the output. The chief beneficiaries of the cereal boom of the early 1980s were the manufacturers of agri-chemicals whose sales in Britain rose from around £100 million to more than £800 million in five years.

Cereal crops 'pushed' for high yields, particularly by early sowing and the application of high levels of nitrogen, are placed under stress and become more vulnerable to disease and competition from weeds. They have to be protected with heavier inputs of fungicides and herbicides. The risk from fungicide-resistant pathogens increases, along with the cost of protection.

But more serious is the fact that nitrate levels in one-third of Britain's soil are over EEC limits and are poisoning the water supply with unpredictable consequences. Before the 1960s very few fertilizers were used and nitrate poisoning was virtually unknown. It takes twenty years for nitrates to percolate through the subsoil, so the effects of today's application of fertilizers on our water supply around the turn of the century could be alarming.

Alongside the environmental effects of agri-business — and cereal production is only one aspect — has been another serious side effect: the flight of people from the land. During the 1970s and early 1980s tenant farmers and livestock producers in Britain were leaving farming at a rate of 5,000 a year. On top of that, farm amalgamations and the mechanization associated with agri-business were making another 5–6,000 farm workers redundant annually.

The Organic Response

It is rare that such a combination of problems — over-production, environmental damage, and unemployment — can be resolved by one solution. But in this case it is so. If Britain were to return on an organized basis to a properly-controlled organic agriculture then all these problems would be minimized. Organic farming, in which growing is based on natural fertilizers and crop rotation, plus a total absence of chemicals and pesticides, produces about 80 per cent of existing yields. This 20 per cent shortfall matches almost perfectly the amount Britain and the EEC generally are over-producing. The environmental problem is overcome because chemical fertilizers and pesticides are abandoned. And the unemployment problem is tackled because organic farming is much more labour intensive than conventional methods.

Coupled with this equation is the fact that demand for organically-grown vegetables and fruit is rising rapidly. In June 1985 a Gallup poll revealed that there were nearly three million people in Britain who were either complete vegetarians or had cut out red meat from their diet. A further 19 million people, a third of the population, had consistently cut their meat consumption, including fish and fowl, over the previous three years. At the same time a number of supermarket chains were predicting that 7 per cent of their fresh vegetable and fruit sales would be organic by 1988, and as much as 25 per cent before the end of the century.

By the early 1980s farmers were beginning to respond, both to this swelling demand and to the environmental consequences of conventional agriculture. The Organic Growers Association of horticulturalists was formed in 1980 and within five years had a membership of 50. British Organic Farmers, an association for larger-scale livestock and cereal farmers, was founded in 1983 and had a membership of 650 two years later. The size of both organizations continues to grow. In 1985 it was estimated that 1 per cent of British farm acreage was taken up by organic producers, and predicted to be 15 per cent by the mid-1990s.

Because they tend to be widely scattered, a problem organic growers have is distributing and marketing their produce. So in 1983 a group of organic farmers in south-west Wales came together and founded Organic Farm Foods. This established a warehouse in Clapham in south London which within two years had achieved a turnover of more than £1 million. During 1985 similar companies were established in Bristol, Birmingham and Edinburgh.

● Pete Segger, chairman of the Organic Growers Association: 'We are on the brink of the biggest upheaval in agriculture this century . . .'
With him is Ginny Mayall who manages the first wholefood warehouse set up in Britain, in Clapham, London.

The chairman of the Organic Growers Association is Pete Segger, a west Wales horticulturist who is also a director of Organic Farm Foods. He believes that farming in Britain is poised for a revolution:

> On the one side we have a situation where demand is falling for the output of the conventional system. The effect is that we are importing more and more specialized foodstuffs, and putting more and more people out of work at home.
>
> On the other hand demand is soaring for the more specialized, high quality organically grown foods, particularly vegetables. We simply can't get enough of them. Demand is outstripping supply. And the more we can, in fact, supply the more people we are going to put back to work on the land — around 20 per cent more people are needed to farm organically-grown produce compared with conventional methods.

The change taking place in British farming has so far been spontaneous. It is happening without any help or intervention from the government. For a farmer to switch from conventional to organic methods is a major decision, involving big losses in the early years. It takes between three and twenty years for land to revert from conventional farming using chemical fertilizer to producing organic produce free of alien constituents. During the transition, yields drop and the farmer cannot win the price benefits that accompany organic produce.

The growing lobby of organic farmers are now pressing for subsidies from the government to cover the transition period, subsidies they say would be more than offset by the benefits accruing to the exchequer from the reductions in surpluses it would have to subvent.

Vested interests, especially from the chemical fertilizer companies; conservatism of the farming establishment; and the bureaucracy of the EEC are all making change along these lines difficult to achieve. But Pete Segger is confident that by the 1990s the pressure for change will be irresistible:

> Agriculture is still in the hands of big businesses and subject to the whims of politicians. But farmers are becoming more and more confused and frightened. For the first time in 20 years people are asking serious questions about food, their health and their environment. We are on the brink of the biggest upheaval in agriculture this century.

The Sunrise Industries

This chapter's examination of the hidden resources in our economy — the wealth inherent in what we have conventionally understood to be 'waste', ranging from sewerage to the contents of our rubbish bins, and the potential of an environmentally managed agriculture — is only a brief exploration of the possibilities. There can be no doubt, however, that boldly tackled with imaginative policies, engaging both central and local government, much could be achieved. Yet the government's policy-makers have ignored the jobs potential in recycling waste and do not see the need for a planned approach. Their attitude must be condemned as wilfully complacent, given the potential that is being ignored. Witness this statement, in the evidence from the Departments of Trade and Industry and Environment to the House of Commons Select Committee on Trade and Industry in 1984, published in its report *The Wealth of Waste:*

> The Government fully recognise the importance of reclamation and recycling and welcome the co-operation between industry,

central and local government, and other bodies with interests in the area. It looks to industry, in its own enlightened self-interest to undertake reclamation/recycling where it makes commercial sense to do so. It does not regard such activities as an end in themselves and consequently has not thought it appropriate to develop a national policy for the sector as a whole.

If such a national policy, to produce wealth and work from waste, were formulated it could be integrated into what John Elkington, director of the environmental campaign Earthlife, has described as the seven Sunrise industries. These are sectors where environmentally compatible and sustainable economic growth in tune with an ecological approach can be advocated. Characteristically they all produce considerably higher value per ton of product than do traditional, and typically declining, manufacturing industry.

The seven, identified by Elkington, are: micro-electronics and information technology; pollution control technology; recycling and resource substitution technology; energy efficiency technology; ecologically tailored energy supply technologies; and the environmental services sector.

It is significant that the potential in the recycling and agricultural initiatives discussed in this chapter at different points touch on most of these headings. Referring to them Elkington commented:

> Even without much government assistance, there is every reason to believe that these seven embryonic industries will contribute considerably more each year to the UK economy by the mid-1990s than will North Sea oil. Unlike fossil fuels, they are based on non-depletable, indefinitely renewable resources, including our imaginative, and other, skills. However, government support (both at the UK and EEC levels) will be vital in building up these industries, given that many of their markets are heavily shaped by government policies and spending . . .

What the initiatives outlined in this chapter have achieved is the creation of practical examples that have proved their case. They have demonstrated that there is the potential in a recycling strategy and a reformed agriculture for generating significant amounts of work and wealth from waste.

Source Guide

Most of the background information on waste and materials

recycling is technical, specialized and difficult to assimilate. The best place to start is with the highly effective pressure group Friends of the Earth which has produced a range of pamphlets and leaflets on the subject: 377 City Road, London EC1V 1NA. Associated with FOE is Earth Resources Research Ltd, a charitable environmental research agency based at 40 James Street, London W1. It has published a book on the background to recycling: *Material Gains,* by Christine Thomas. A more up-to-date and unusually accessible analysis is the House of Commons Trade and Industry Committee report *The Wealth of Waste,* published in 1984 and available from HMSO. A comprehensive account of how recycling waste can create work in developing countries is contained in Jon Vogler's book *Work from Waste,* published in 1983 by Intermediate Technology Publications, 9 King Street, London WC2.

The Taunton Think Tank's report *Jobs Not Waste* can be obtained from PO Box 135, Taunton, Somerset TA1 2NG. To keep in touch with contemporary developments in waste, recycling and renewable energy issues there is no better way than subscribing to the monthly newpaper *Warmer Bulletin — warmth and energy from rubbish,* available from Warmer Campaign, Wadhurst, East Sussex TN5 6NR.

Resourcesaver and its associated companies can be contacted at Anderson's Building, St John's Street, Bedminster, Bristol BS3.

One company researching in the field of microbe treatment of waste and production of methane is Biotechnica Ltd, 5 Chiltern Close, Cardiff CF4 5DL. WMC Resource Recovery Ltd, is based at 2 Eaton Crescent, Clifton, Bristol BS8 2EJ. For further details of the project for converting waste into oil contact Noel McAuliffe, professor of Inorganic Chemistry, University of Manchester Institute of Science and Technology.

For information on the organic growing movement in Britain the primary contact is the Soil Association, which publishes a quarterly review, at Walnut Tree Manor, Haughly, Suffolk 1P14 3RS. The Organic Growers Association can be contacted at Aeron Park, Llangeitho, Tregaron, Dyfed; and British Organic Farmers at Leggatts Park, Potters Bar, Hertfordshire. Between them these two associations publish a bi-monthly magazine, *New Farmer and Grower — Britain's Journal of Organic Food Production.*

The environmental campaign Earthlife which publishes a magazine, *Earthlife News,* is based at 10 Belgrave Square, London SW1X 8PH. John Elkington's *Seven Bridges to the Future:*

Industrial Growth Points for a Sustainable Economy is contained in *The Conservation and Development Programme for the UK: A Response to the World Conservation Strategy,* 1983. This is available, along with a popular version of the strategy itself, *How to Save the World,* from Kogan Page Ltd, 120 Pentonville Road, London N1 9JN.

5. Business Ecology

The social responsibility of management used to be the last gasp
paragraph of the chairman's statement. It is now beginning to be
recognised as inextricably involved in everything to do with good
management. The manager cannot be separated from human
problems. He cannot be brutally effective and rich anymore . . .
— Quoted by Francis Kinsman in *The New Agenda*.

In chapter 2 the importance of community initiatives and
regenerating the local economy was described as a major aspect
of the 'new economics'. What is particularly significant is the
evidence that the thrust of the argument is being understood and
acted upon by mainstream business and industry. The rapid
growth of Business in the Community during the 1980s, by now
involving some 2,500 companies in the work of local enterprise
trusts, is the clearest indication. Another was the establishment
in the early 1980s of Local Initiative Support (UK) by a number
of large companies — notably British Petroleum, Baxi Heating,
Shell, and Provincial Insurance — aimed at channelling investment
into community enterprises. It quickly established an investment
fund whose primary purpose is 'to maximize local responsibility
and local control over local resources in the interests of local
economic development'. The experience of rebuilding local
economies in both Britain and America, say the organizers, has
produced two crucially important lessons:

- Run-down areas will not be revitalized by either the public
  or private sector acting alone, but by a collaborative approach
  that recognizes that success depends, in part, upon enabling
  local people to have a stake in the future prosperity of their
  locality.
- Local initiatives need to secure assets under their control to
  provide a local asset base and thus become less dependent
  on grants and subsidies.

The work of Local Initiative Support (UK), as with Business in the Community and other similar ventures is freely acknowledged to arise out of enlightened self-interest. In the case of Local Initiative Support (UK) this perception is born from a shrewd analysis of investment trends and the inter-dependence of business activity. So far as investment is concerned perhaps the outstanding feature of the twenty years spanning the 1960s to the 1980s is the increasing proportion that has become managed and directed by large financial institutions such as the banks, the pension funds and the insurance companies. Between them they now invest between £15-20 billion a year, divided almost evenly between insurance companies and pension funds. But by their very nature these are institutions which can have no personal attachment to any particular investment locality.

At the same time broad economic circumstances — such as new technology, world competition, and the scarcity and expense of basic commodities — has led to the decline, and in some cases collapse, of traditional industries like coal, steel, textiles and ship-building. Moreover, as these industries have tended to be concentrated in specific parts of the country — notably in Wales, the North of England and Scotland — their decline has led to the creation of areas of dereliction and multiple deprivation. And this process has been accelerated by the financial institutions which have tended to withdraw investment money, just because these areas are in decline, and re-direct it instead into property investment on 'prime' sites.

But, as Financial Initiative Support (UK) points out:

> The growth of areas of multiple deprivation increasingly threaten the financial basis on which the institutional investors depend. The search for 'safe' areas becomes more and more difficult, like looking for sandbanks to stand on in a rising sea.
>
> In reality, commercial and industrial development is based upon a network of supporting economic and social activities, which are in turn dependent on the people who live and work in the locality. As with farming, the economic soil is a compost that supports growth and vitality. If small-scale organic activity is destroyed by a lack of sustenance and heavy cropping, the result is dependency followed by breakdown.
>
> The durability of the local economy *in its entirety* is, therefore, of fundamental importance not only to the local people but also to the investor. The long-term concentration of resources on one part to the detriment of the rest will distort the system and may, in time, lead to its breakdown. Sustaining local economies in a

broad sense should, in contrast, lead in the medium to long-term to a higher overall rate of return on investment.

What is slowly developing in the traditionally pragmatic, harsh and competitive business world is a concern with industry's environmental impact, with co-operation, and with the idea of socially useful as well as profitable production. Taken together these can be fairly described as an ecological approach to business. Examples of the approach in action can be found on the ground in the three key areas of business activity — finding a place to work, establishing a market, and raising finance. It would be wrong to over-emphasize the extent to which business ecology is becoming a major motivating force in commerce and industry. Nevertheless, the activities described below demonstrate what is possible. And if their advocates are right, the principles of business ecology will be increasingly applied, not out of altruistic sentiment but because they make sound economic sense.

The New Work Trust

The most fundamental requirement for the success of a new business is that a market should exist or be created for its product or service. However, the most immediate problem facing many small firms starting up is simply finding somewhere to work that is not too much of a drain on resources. The most common response to this need has been the creation of managed workshops, often by local authorities, in which more than one firm is accommodated under one roof sharing a variety of facilities. By the mid-1980s there were about sixty such workshops around the country. One of the best examples, certainly in the range of services and activities it has brought together, is the New Work Trust in Bristol. Housed in a former factory, warehouse and school it is another illustration of what can be developed when local government and established businesses co-operate, exploiting funds provided by central government in the process. As so often in three enterprises, too, the catalyst is an individual whose energy, flair and entrepreneurial drive has done most to ensure the project's success. In this case it is Mike Winwood, managing director of the New Work Trust and formerly a lecturer in Social Administration at the University of Bristol.

It is instructive to trace briefly the development of the New Work Trust since it shows how, from very small beginnings, a community can create its own employment and business

● Mike Winwood, managing director of the Bristol New Work Trust, seen on the upper floor of the workshops, a converted factory — 'A holistic approach is absolutely essential . . .'

institutions. In December 1980 the then chairman of Kingswood District Council, in south-east Bristol, held a reception where he remarked on the growing unemployment in the area and speculated whether it was time people in the locality got together to try and do something about it, though he confessed he had little idea how to approach the problem in practical terms. One person who heard his remarks was Mike Winwood who set about making contact with businessmen in the area. In June 1981 the New Work Trust was launched at a public meeting as a local development agency focusing on newstart business creation.

Interestingly the strategy, from the start, was to avoid reliance on direct subsidies in any long-term sense. The objective was to make the venture self-supporting and this was achieved remarkably quickly. Finance was raised from a variety of sources:

1. The private sector in Bristol came up with a one-off injection of £32,000 pump-priming investment, with twenty-two firms participating. The main initiative came from the Barclays Bank Social Responsibility Fund which offered £15,000 provided it was matched pound for pound by other businesses in the city.

2. Commercial borrowing with a £20,000 overdraft secured by British Imperial Tobacco and a £70,000 loan secured by the Department of Industry.
3. Conversion of the factory was helped by some investment by the landlord together with subsidized labour by workers on a Manpower Services community project.

The workshops, with space for eighty small units, opened in September 1981. Over the first year capital costs totalled £160,000 but at the end of the year the project was breaking even, and by the end of the third year making a profit with a revenue turnover of £760,000.

The project had the advantage of the area it was born in: though there was 11 per cent unemployment it was a relatively buoyant area of a buoyant city in a buoyant part of Britain. Moreover, there was a high and diversified level of skills in the labour market, for example in precision engineering, leatherwork, clothing and footwear. A major problem, however, was that small premises and business back-up services were in short supply.

By mid-1985 the New Work Trust had accommodated 143 firms, 40 per cent of which had already started to trade before coming to the workshops. Of the total, sixty firms were still with the venture, eleven had failed, and the rest had grown and developed and moved out to bigger premises. Between them they had created 260 new jobs in broadly three categories of industry:

● Traditional activities such as engineering, sheet metal, clothing manufacture, printing, the timber trade and cabinet making.
● Professional, office-based business such as civil engineering and computer software supplies.
● New technology such as optical engineering, lens-making and polishing, and electronics.

Despite the many advantages of the project, most notably the relatively prosperous area in which it took root, the outstanding reason for its success has been the unique combination of initiatives it put together which were of immediate benefit to the small firms attracted to it:

1. *The workshops.* The 80 units established were organized on an open-plan basis on two floors of the converted factory so their size can be expanded or contracted according to

demand. Heavier industry is on the ground floor, with the office and generally quieter activities on the first floor.

2. *Business back-up.* Collective services are provided such as typing, front office message-taking and telephone answering, photocopying, a group telex, word processing and data processing. The objective is to allow small firms to benefit from modern management and technology, reduce their administrative burden and improve their business control.

3. *Training.* The initial thrust was in the area of business information technology with more than 200 people benefitting in the first three years. Alongside this, a similar number of school leavers were recruited and trained at the workshops, having the advantage of on-site practical experience with a wide variety of manufacturing activities. In turn they provide a ready source of skilled labour for expanding firms.

4. *Marketing.* In a separate building, a former primary school, the Trust has created its Small Firms Marketing Centre which, when it opened in 1983, was the first of its kind in Britain. By now its example is being followed elsewhere. Full-time, expert staff act as consultants to small firms, talking through with them their marketing problems and providing practical suggestions for reaching customers. In its first two years more than 1,000 firms used the Centre.

5. *Networking.* Under contract with the Manpower Services Commission, work began in September 1981 to create a profile of small firm activity in the locality, broadly defined as north-east Avon. Three years later 4,200 small firms — companies employing less than fifty people — had been identified and brought together under the umbrella of Business Link, a network association. At the same time a Supporters Club of 260 larger firms, banks and insurance companies, was established so there could be an interchange of advice, particularly management and technical support, and also a trade directory for the provision of locally-based goods and services for industry.

Mike Winwood believes that, though the circumstances of other areas of the country are different, there are lessons that can be drawn from the experience of the Bristol New Work Trust:

Our outstanding achievement has been to bring together, in a unique combination, facilities and back-up services for small firms starting up in business. It's common sense really. If a firm has got a financial problem, that is bound to affect their marketing strategy. Both of these will, in turn, affect their production pattern and quality control. If, on the other hand, a firm starts with a quality control problem, that is going to affect their ability to deliver their goods and satisfy their customers. The probability then is that they will end up with a cash-flow problem.

It can seem that any one of these problems are isolated and can be dealt with as such. But the truth is that sooner or later they all impinge upon one another. A holistic approach is absolutely essential and that is what we have attempted to put into practice.

Raising Money

There is little doubt that the long-term survival and expansion of any commercial initiative is bound up with what is loosely described as marketing. Unless it can establish a secure demand and market for its product, whether, it be goods or services, and can devise efficient ways of distributing and promoting it, no enterprise can hope to prosper.

Having said that, the biggest problem most small firms face when they are at the point of getting off the ground is raising money. This is particularly the case with most new enterprises in the alternative economic sector described in previous chapters. Whenever conventional financial institutions contemplate making a loan, classically they want to be reassured that the borrower has a reasonable track record, has a properly developed business plan, can guarantee an acceptable rate of return in interest on the investment, and, above all, can provide good security for the advance.

All of these are conditions which most new firms starting up find difficult to satisfy, let alone those in the alternative sector where, by definition, many of these conditions simply cannot be met in any pure sense. Beyond this there is no doubt that the venture capital market in Britain is poorly developed, a fact recognized by the government. In 1981 it instituted a Loan Guarantee Scheme whereby the Department of Industry will secure 80 per cent of an advance to a new small business, leaving the remaining risk to be picked up by the banks. Another government initiative, begun in 1982 is the New Enterprise Allowance Scheme, designed to encourage unemployed people to set up their own businesses: you have to be able to invest £1,000 in the enterprise and to have been unemployed for at least thirteen weeks to qualify for an allowance of £40 a week for up to a year.

Co-operatives have particular problems in raising money, partly because conventional financial institutions remain sceptical about their methods of organization and partly because the constitution of most worker co-operatives specifically prevents the issuing of shares. In this area private enterprise and the conventional money markets have left a vacuum that has been largely filled by local authorities, acting through the local Co-operative Development Agencies, discussed in chapter 2. The funds have been made available under the Inner Urban Areas Act of 1978 for the inner-cities and, more generally but more parsimoniously, by invoking the power to spend up to the product of a 2p rate, given to local authorities by Section 137 of the Local Government Act of 1972.

Nowhere have these powers been more imaginatively employed than in London. Fourteen of the London boroughs have created their own Co-operative Development Agencies which offer small start-up grants of around £1,000 and rent-free allowances on workshops while the Greater London Enterprise Board, under the auspices of the Greater London Council, spawned the London Co-operative Enterprise Board which awards grants of up to £25,000. Using these funds and agencies some seventy co-operatives were set up in the borough of Hackney alone in the first half of the 1980s. A member of the Anarres Video Co-operative in Hackney's Bradbury Street, Kevin Sheridan, said raising money is the overriding problem most co-operatives have:

> We approached the banks to get finance and, although we did a lot of work for them they were unaware of our needs — I think they were unaware of even what a co-operative was — and in the end we got no help from them at all. We got some help from our local Co-operative Development Agency, particularly legal advice about setting up. Financially we got most help from the Greater London Enterprise Board which have established easy-term loans for people in our position.

Despite the major initiatives for financing new enterprises, especially worker co-operatives, coming from the public sector, there are signs of a growing awareness in the private sector that the principles of business ecology can be applied, and applied profitably, in the venture capital field. Three agencies are profiled below and, though their operations are small, they illustrate the possibilities.

● Kevin Sheridan, of the Anarres Video Co-opertive in Hackney's Bradbury Street: 'The banks were unaware of our needs — I don't think they knew what a co-operative was . . .'

Industrial Common Ownership Finance (ICOF)

This agency grew out of the Industrial Common Ownership Movement discussed in chapter 3 and was established as a separate company in 1974. It received a major boost in 1976 when the Industrial Common Ownership Act provided £250,000 as a basis for a revolving fund. Since then ICOF has received a further £500,000 from the West Midlands County Council to lend to co-operatives in its area.

In mid-1985 ICOF had £400,000 on loan to fifty-five co-

● Mary Asfour, development officer with Industrial Common Ownership Finance: 'The established finance institutions are not used to the idea of enterprises where people pool their skills, commitment and energy rather than their financial resources, and are accountable to each other for their decisions . . .'

operatives, giving an average loan of some £7,000. These are relatively small sums, but vital amounts for the kind of firms being set up by the new wave of worker co-operatives in the 1980s. For example, the three co-operatives featured in chapter 3 — Treeworks, Happy Hands, and Soft Solution — were all part-funded by ICOF. As one of ICOF's development officers, Mary Asfour, based in Bristol, explained:

> Worker co-operatives require specialist assistance because they represent a different dimension in the business world. ICOF recognises that in a common ownership, the people are the business. The established finance institutions are not used to the idea of enterprises where people pool their skills, commitment and energy rather than their financial resources, and are

accountable to each other for their decisions.

In addition to this, in the current unemployment situation there are many unemployed people — women, gay people, ethnic minorities and the disabled — who find it especially difficult to put together the financial back-up to act as security with the banks. ICOF, on the other hand, makes a point of doing all it can to help such disadvantaged groups.

ICOF is controlled by a board of ten directors, known as trustees, who are drawn from the co-operative sector — the Co-operative Development Agencies, the Co-operative Bank, ICOM, the trade union movement and local government. As well as obtaining money from central and local government ICOF has received funds in the form of gifts and grants from individuals and trusts.

However, under the terms of the Banking Acts, ICOF cannot act as a deposit-taking agency, accepting money for on-lending to co-operative enterprises. Despite this activity being carried out in one form or another by the Co-operative Bank, the Co-operative Development Agency in London, and local authorities, there is a need for a fully-fledged Co-operative Investment Bank to build on and extend the work of ICOF. It would act, in effect, as a banker of last resort, though often putting in some of its own money to bring in and encourage others. Its task would be to work out the most favourable financial package, with contributions on the best terms that could be negotiated from merchant banks, pension funds, ordinary banks and other specialized financial institutions.

Mercury Provident

The Mercury Provident Society, a licensed deposit-taking institution under the 1979 Banking Act, was set up in 1974 with the deliberate objective of dealing with money in a new way. Its directors are chartered accountants, solicitors, bankers, surveyors and other professional people. They all have in common an adherence to the ideas of Rudolph Steiner, an Austrian philospher who lived between 1861 and 1925. His thinking, which centres on an overall vision of the person as a spiritual being, has been applied in many practical ways, from biodynamic organic farming to educational theory, and Mercury Provident investments reflect these concerns. But as well as this, the Society aims to bring investors into a new relationship with the projects into which their money is put. It matches specific investors with specific projects and investors decide their own rate of return, within a range of 0 to 8 per cent. As the Society itself puts it:

> Many people who make bank deposits feel dissatisfied at knowing little of how their investment monies are used. It is not possible for them to be involved in the bank's investment decisions. Mercury encourages depositors to influence the way in which their deposits are applied. It seeks to bring the depositor and borrower together so that each is aware of the other's intentions and purposes . . .
>
> Mercury's task often includes business counselling as people setting out on new ventures need sound advice in handling assets and money. Thus Mercury often brings ordinary business criteria to bear in judging a project, but this in itself is not sufficient; it also looks for the impulse inspiring the project to sense whether it is altruistic, responds to the urgent needs of the times and works for the future benefit of mankind . . .

By 1985, after a little over ten years of trading, Mercury Provident had invested some £1.2m in around 100 projects with between 40 and 50 being developed. It had more than 2,000 investors on its mailing list and was expanding. The Society has developed a novel method of creating security for a loan where borrowers cannot provide collateral by themselves. This involves the borrower finding a group of people who support the project to act as guarantors to the loan. Mercury Provident sees this approach as additional evidence justifying the investment it recommends:

> Not only do guarantors represent an act of community support for the ideal behind the project, but they are an act of confidence in the capacities of individuals who are taking the initiative, and they are a way of offering both financial and human support to the project.

One venture that used this method of securing the loan it negotiated with Mercury Provident was the Treeworks co-operative described in chapter 3. One of its members, John Emery, described their efforts at raising money as initially one of frustration:

> Setting up a business always takes longer than you think it's going to and the early years are precisely the moment when you need

a flexible lender — willing to allow you favourable interest rates or even defer or waive payments if necessary. But this is just the moment when the conventional institutions are least likely to accommodate you in this way.

We spent a lot of time going to the traditional sources of finance such as the banks, without a great deal of success. Of the various schemes sponsored by the central government, the only one really applicable to us was the Loan Guarantee Scheme. But this is very expensive for a small firm like ourselves, costing, in fact, about 2 to 3 per cent more than would be charged a large company.

But our main problem was that we could not personally secure any loans.

● John Emery, of the Treeworks co-operative, working with a power saw, part of the substantial investment put into the business: 'Without the alternative sources of finance we were able to put together I doubt if we could have established ourselves at all . . .'

This was where Mercury Provident came in. It found Treeworks its initial £10,000 of investment, guaranteed by a number of people who knew the business and were willing to support it by securing varying amounts of the loan, varying between £50 and £5,000. Once the co-operative was under way and needed more money to expand, particularly money to finance an electric kiln to dry timber, ICOF stepped in with a £10,000 loan and also helped Treeworks negotiate a further £30,000 from the Avon Co-operative Development Agency.

Treeworks is now a flourishing business. It has found a definite niche in the woodland management market, it has a committed and dedicated workforce, and it has good prospects of expanding. Yet in its early days the chances of it being funded by the conventional financial institutions was remote. As John Emery put it:

> Without the alternative sources of finance we were able to put together I doubt if we would have established ourselves at all. The existing financial set up does not help small businesses in general get off the ground and it certainly does not help co-operatives.

Another venture supported by Mercury Provident is the Centre for Employment Initiatives described in chapter 2. It has invested £25,000 to enable the Centre to expand its publishing activities, again with a community of guarantors. One of the Centre's director's, Colin Ball, described their relationship with Mercury Provident in the following terms:

> There are two reasons why we are linking with the Mercury. The first is plain, straightforward necessity — we can't find anybody in the traditional sector to give us the capital we need. Four banks have turned us down because they say they don't understand our operation.
>
> The other reason, and this ultimately is more important, is that there is a philosophical coincidence of ideas between ourselves and Mercury. We are a not-for-profit organisation and as we're not seeking any personal profit out of what we do, we tend to expect those who are investing money with us to share this objective, rather than seeking purely commercial rates of return. I suppose this is why the banks don't understand us and Mercury Provident does.

The Financial Initiative

Partly because of its status under the Banking Acts, and partly because of its low interest loans policy, Mercury Provident does not operate in the high risk venture capital market where big returns can be expected as a reward for imaginative, intuitive investment. And, indeed, this business area might not be thought especially amenable to the application of ecological business principles. However, in 1983 a number of businessmen — some of them connected with Mercury Provident — launched The Financial Initiative Ltd, described as 'Britain's first "ethical" investment management company'. It aims at investments of between £15,000 and £100,000 in companies that may not have a strong track record but which are judged to have ecologically sound objectives and committed people running them. Unlike Mercury Provident, Financial Initiative also aims to become highly involved in the day-to-day management of the companies it invests in.

Early investments included a £15,000 equity share in Real Organic Gardening Ltd, a Kent company supplying organic gardening products such as composts, soil dressings and non-toxic pesticides; and a £22,000 equity investment in Caledonian International Ambulances Ltd, a Gatwick company specializing in repatriating ill and injured people from abroad. Other projects being evaluated included a wholefood shop and restaurant; a woodlands management service; a holistic health centre; book publishing and video publishing companies; and a software house specializing in telecomputing systems with school and home applications.

The objective in all these cases was to match enterprises which require equity finance with people wishing to invest in what Financial Initiative describes as ecologically worthwhile projects:

> People are increasingly coming to realise that many of the supposedly wealth-creating practices of recent years are in fact impoverishing both society and the environment. Many people now see poverty and starvation, disease and pollution, as being greatly exacerbated by practices adopted only for quick profit, and initiated for individual or sectional gain, which diminish human dignity, deplete natural resources, damage the environment, and detract from the interests of the community as a whole.
>
> Only when the good of the whole is respected in economic activities is real wealth created. It is destroyed by the depletion

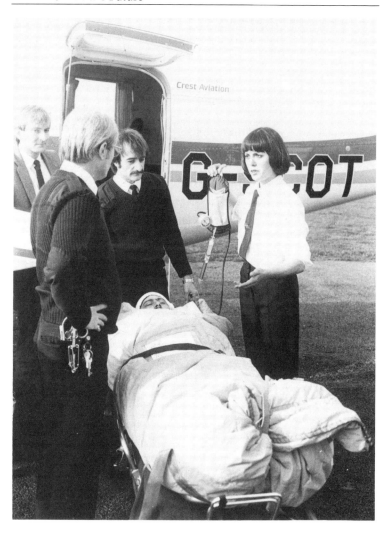

● Caledonian International Ambulances — one of the enterprises funded by The Financial Initiative. Its founder, Sister Jackie McDougall (on the right in picture) commented: 'We went to the large financial institutions and found that the sum we were looking for was too small for them. In fact, they didn't appear interested in risk capital for start-up businesses at all . . .'

of natural resources, the destruction of the environment and the diminution of human dignity or potential. While practices with such effects may increase short-term sectional profit, this is at disproportionate, long-term and often irreversible cost to the larger ecological or human community.

As a declaration of the fundamental principles of business ecology this statement could not be bettered.

Socially Useful Production

This discussion of the idea of business ecology has so far focused on how its approach relates to the immediate problems that face enterprises when they are starting up: finding a place to work, developing a market, and raising finance. But underlying all these questions is the more fundamental one of what is business about in the first place? What is the relationship between a business's product, the profit motive, and job creation? The answer business ecology provides is: socially useful production.

The concept has been most clearly developed in practical terms during the 1980s by the Greater London Council operating through the independent company it set up in July 1982, the Greater London Enterprise Board. The background was straightforward unemployment — one in eight of London's workforce was unemployed. Manufacturing jobs had been especially hard-hit by the impact of the recession, de-industrialization and de-skilling. By the end of 1982, the total number of jobs in the GLC area was only two-fifths of what it had been in 1962. At the same time, London's people confronted a mass of unmet needs — in housing, health and the quality of their lives. Yet factories were closing, machinery was being sold off for scrap, and the city owned 33 million square feet of unused factory space. The response was succinctly summarized by the GLC in its 1983 booklet *Jobs For A Change:*

> What is required is a new economic guide. In the GLC we are trying to spell one out. We start not from profit but from unused resources, and our guide is not just the market but social need. It is quite simple: to find the vacant land and buildings, the knocked down machinery, the stranded skills and energies of London's workforce, and — with financial support — to bring them together to rebuild our wealth-creating industries and to produce what the great majority of us so clearly need: proper housing, health, and transport.

That such a perspective should come from a local authority is entirely understandable, since in contrast with a private business, it has to take into account wider considerations than simply 'return on capital invested'. Even so, a major influence on GLC thinking was the experience during the 1970s of the Lucas Aerospace Workers whose combined shop stewards' committee produced an alternative corporate plan for the company. The plan, published in 1976, was a response to threatened redundancies and an effort to persuade the company to shift away from armaments production towards the production of socially useful goods. When published the plan comprised six documents, each of about 200 pages, containing technical details, engineering drawings, costings and supporting economic data for around 150 new products. They included alternative energy sources; new transport systems (such as a vehicle usable on road or rail); medical equipment (for example, kidney machines and aids for the blind); and machinery for safe working under the sea, in mining and fire-fighting.

That the Lucas Aerospace alternative plan has had a direct influence on GLC policy is shown by the following quotation from the Labour Party manifesto produced for the GLC elections in 1981:

> Groups of workers such as the Lucas Aerospace Shop Stewards Committee have begun to develop ideas on alternative production — using technologies which interact with human skills; making goods which are conducive to human health and welfare; working in ways which conserve, rather than waste resources.

In pursuit of these objectives the Greater London Enterprise Board spent £3.5m setting up a series of technology networks based on polytechnics in London: a New Technology Network; an Energy and Employment Network, a Transport Technology Network; and two area networks based on north-east and south-east London. These operate by bringing together community and workplace groups with academics and researchers, providing workshop space to develop prototypes, and injecting pump-priming finance to get projects into a position to attract more conventional financial backing.

In its first two years, applying the principles of socially useful production together with funding new worker co-operatives plus a number of rescue operations, the Enterprise Board saved or created a total of 2,322 jobs. The cost worked out at about £3,500 per job — half the average cost to the taxpayer of an unemployed person in benefits and lost taxes, and far lower than the £10,000 investment cost per job which the government set for its regional grants programme at the time. The Director of the GLEB Technology Division, Mike Cooley, formerly a member of the Lucas Aerospace Combine Committee, outlined their approach to socially useful production in graphic terms:

● Mike Cooley, of the Greater London Enterprise Board, riding the Pedelec electric bicycle, one of its socially useful product developments: 'We are alarmed at the way many new technologies are being introduced specifically to deskill and displace human beings . . .'

It seems to me as a technologist that there is something seriously wrong when we can develop forms of science and technology that can guide a missile to another continent with an accuracy of a few metres, and yet the blind and disabled are staggering around London in much the same way as in medieval times. It seems to me irresponsible that we deliberately set out to design cars that fall apart after four or five years, or that 3,000 people die every year in Britain because they cannot get a kidney machine that in technological terms is extremely simple to make.

We've been working on ideas for a portable kidney dialysis machine that is simple to make and yet a life-saving system that gives the patient the dignity of being active and mobile. We have developed a heat pump which works like a refrigerator in reverse, drawing in energy from outside a building and creating significant savings in energy costs. We're developing a power assisted bicycle to encourage more people to cycle. And we're working on a body structure for cars to enable them to be easily repaired and last for more than 15 years.

We are alarmed at the way many new technologies are being introduced specifically to deskill and displace human beings. We freely admit that there are certain jobs which are boring, hazardous, routine or dangerous and which probably should be automated out of existence. But we do not think it correct to do that universally. We are looking at ways of designing systems that build on human knowledge and intelligence and help people, rather than the other way around.

Encouraging the Small Enterprise

There is little doubt that the principles of business ecology are more easily put into practice with small firms rather than large. And the job creation trends in this respect are encouraging. In the ten years to 1985, firms employing less than 100 people created 52 per cent of all new jobs, and those with less than 20 people created 31 per cent. In total, these small firms notched up a net gain of 1.8 million new jobs, while larger firms showed a loss of 1.2 million.

The smaller the firm the more chance the individual will feel a sense of involvement and responsibility in its progress. Industrial psychologists have established that the highest productivity per person is achieved by teams of between seven and fifteen people. Small firms also score through flexibility, since demand is growing for individualistic, specialized goods rather than cheaper mass-produced products which tend to be imported in any event.

More and more people are attempting to start up on their own: between 1980 and 1983, for instance, 640,000 people in Britain registered for VAT. Yet, in the same period 520,000 went out of business, giving a net gain of just 120,000. The fact is that around 100,000 small firms fold each year and one in four fail during the first five critical years of operation.

This chapter's discussion of the concept of business ecology has demonstrated ways in which these figures could be improved. Perhaps the major lesson is in dealing with money. New job-generating firms tend to be small and dynamic and the conventional financial institutions, notably the banks, tend to regard them negatively — as untried and unstable. A business ecological approach, however, tends to take a different view, as Financial Initiative's chief executive, Giles Chitty, explained:

● Giles Chitty, Financial Initiative's chief executive: 'What we tend to focus on is how we assess the aspirations and the quality of the people . . .

On the whole the traditional venture capital companies in this country want to see a track record that is quantifiable on paper. They want to see a success record which obviously implies a major reduction in their apparent risk.

What we tend to focus on much more is how we assess the aspirations and the quality of the people — not just as skilled managers or skilled technicians, but in terms of their commitment to what they are trying to do, their willingness to work with people on an open basis, their integrity and their sense of the ecological value of the service or product they are producing. These, of course, are less quantifiable than records of profit and loss, sales and output. But in our experience its always the people who are the key to success and where we need to apply our judgement and intuition most.

Source Guide

Compared with the United States the concept of business ecology is poorly developed in Britain, a fact illustrated by the poverty of literature on the subject. A good starting point, however, is a survey of leading industrialists, trade unionists and academics carried out during 1983 by financial journalist Francis Kinsman. His report entitled *The New Agenda* is published by Spencer Stuart Management Consultants, Brook House, 113 Park Lane, London W1. Kinsman is a founder member of The Business Network, created in 1982 'to foster a holistic approach to business which integrates the needs of the individual and the environment.' It holds seminars, publishes a newsletter, and promotes new business initiatives. It is based at 18 Well Walk, London NW3.

Enquiries concerning Local Initiative Support (UK) should be made to its secretary, Stan Windass, at The Rookery, Adderbury, Banbury, Oxon. It has published an interesting prospectus of the ventures around Britain it is actively supporting, each of which illustrates in different ways the ideas of business ecology outlined in this chapter. One of them is the New Work Trust, based at Avondale Workshops, Woodland Way, Bristol.

The Directory of Social Change (based at 9 Mansfield Place, London NW3 1HS) has published a series of comprehensive guides on raising money from industry, government, and trusts and also on industrial sponsorship and joint promotions.

Industrial Common Ownership Finance is based at 4 Giles Street, Northampton NN1 1AA. As well as funding co-operatives it offers a consultancy service and publishes a monthly newsletter.

The Greater London Enterprise Board has published a useful booklet on funding for worker co-operatives, *A Strategy for Co-operation,* available from GLEB, Co-ops Unit, Structural Investment Division, 63–67 Newington Causeway, London SE1 6BD. The Co-operative Bank is based at PO Box 101, 1 Balloon Street, Manchester, M60 4EP.

The Mercury Provident Society can be contacted at Orlingbury House, Lewes Road, Forest Row, Sussex RH18 5AA. It has published a pamphlet on its activities and philosophy, *Dealing With Money Consciously,* and also produces a regular newsletter for investors. The Ecology Building Society, set up to lend on energy saving and other ecological properties and schemes, is based at 43 Main Street, Cross Hills, Keighley, West Yorkshire BD20 8TT. The Financial Initiative's headquarters are Yondover House, Stratford Toney, Salisbury, Wiltshire SP5 4AT.

An analysis of the Greater London Enterprise Board's activities has been published by Dave Elliott, director of the Open University Technology Policy Group, *The GLC's Innovation and Employment Initiatives,* available from Faculty of Technology, Open University, Walton Hall, Milton Keynes, MK7 6AA. GLEB itself has published a number of background pamphlets on its technology networks.

A full account of the Lucas Aerospace alternative plan is contained in *The Lucas Plan* by Hilary Wainwright and Dave Elliott (Alison and Busby, 1982). Mike Cooley has outlined his ideas on socially useful production in *Architect or Bee? The human/technology relationship* published by Langley Technical Services, 95 Sussex Place, Slough, SL1 1NN.

An up-to-date and comprehensive account of the concept of socially useful production is contained in *Very Nice Work If You Can Get It: The Socially Useful Production Debate*, edited by Collective Design/Projects and published by Spokesman, Bertrand Russell House, Gamble Street, Nottingham.

6. *Transition to a New Economy*

> We are in a transition stage. Just as during the Industrial Revolution there were profound changes in employment patterns focussed principally on the shift from agriculture to manufacturing, so today there is a shift from manufacturing to the service industries in general and the knowledge industries in particular . . . The outlines of the major industry of the 21st Century, the 'human relations and psychological satisfaction' industry, begin to emerge.
> — Tom Stonier in *The Wealth of Information*

In the hundred years to the 1980s at least five upheavals can be traced which, in accelerating progression, have caused major changes to the economy and employment. They are:

- The post-1880 agricultural revolution with the mechanization of farming;
- The industrial revolution with the mechanization of manufacturing;
- The entry of many more women into the labour force;
- The energy price rises of the 1970s;
- The information revolution of the 1980s.

On each occasion it has been predicted that the forthcoming technological or social revolution would result in a huge rise in unemployment. On each occasion up to the 1980s these predictions proved wrong. During the century employment actually tripled. Every five-year period, except the early 1930s, saw an increase in the proportion of the population employed. And this even applied during the 1970s, despite the oil price rises near the beginning and end of the decade.

Looking at the first major change, in which the proportion of the labour force working on the land dropped from more than half at the end of the last century to less than 5 per cent today, a number of factors eased the transition. First, the change was gradual because, initially at least, there was no large-scale imports of food. Second, the re-training necessary to take up factory jobs proved modest. Third, the willingness to be mobile — to leave the land for the cities — proved large.

As workers flooded from the land into the factories there were fears that mechanization would soon replace them. Instead, low-cost mass production created mass markets and by the early 1900s industrial employment exceeded all others. During the twentieth century, however, the proportion of manufacturing jobs have steadily declined, from around 50 per cent in the early years to around 30 per cent by the early 1980s, being replaced by jobs in the service sector. All the predictions say that the proportion employed in manufacturing are due to plunge before the end of the century, to perhaps as little as 10 per cent. Automation will mean that, in the same way as a tiny proportion of the labour force today produces the food needed, a comparable proportion will satisfy demand for manufactured goods. The question is: will there be sufficient new jobs in the service and information technology sectors of the economy to take up the slack?

Between the 1880s and 1980s, the proportion of working-age women in paid employment soared from around 10 per cent to 44 per cent, with the likelihood that before the end of the century there will be more women in paid employment than men. Until now new jobs, such as secretaries, telephone operators and teachers, have been added and expanded and women have been painlessly absorbed into the labour market — not least because they were generally willing to accept lower wages. However, in future it is likely that women will compete more directly with men in the new jobs emerging in the information technology field, and highly unlikely that they will be prepared to continue to accept lower wages.

The rise in oil prices in the 1970s did not have the impact on employment that many feared. It did, however, precipitate a world recession which hastened the shake-out of manufacturing jobs. Consumption of oil generally reduced and, in Britain's case, North Sea oil further complicated any assessment of the impact of changes in energy prices on job prospects. What seems clear, however, is that the cost of non-renewable resources like oil will continue upwards over the long term and make the prospect for economic recovery and job creation more difficult.

Taken together, all the trends appear to point emphatically to the need for far fewer conventional jobs in the future. So will the fifth upheaval described above, the information revolution, fulfil the fears of mass unemployment that eluded the other changes outlined? Indeed, can it be said to be happening already with around four million unemployed in the Britain of the mid-1980s?

There are four main employment sectors and their relative importance in terms of the number of people they employ is well illustrated by Charles Handy in the following diagram reproduced from his book *The Future of Work:*

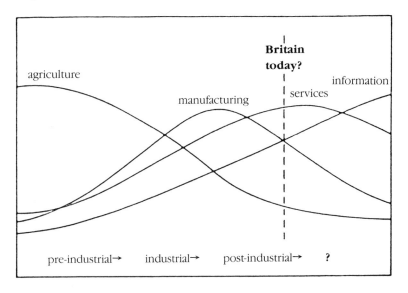

The trends illustrated are confirmed by the following figures for the main sectors in Britain up to 1981:

- Jobs in agriculture and mining went *down* from 1.7 million in 1961 to 0.9 million in 1981 (4 per cent of the total);
- Jobs in manufacturing and construction went *down* from 10.2 million in 1976 to 7.6 million in 1981 (33.5 per cent of the total);
- Jobs in the service sector — state services such as health and education, as well as private service industries like banking and retailing — went *up* from 11.4 million in 1961 to 14.7

million in 1981 (an astonishing 63 per cent of the total).

- There are no official statistics yet available for the information sector, a sub-division of the service sector which includes all activities which process information. But informed estimates indicate that it is the most rapidly growing sector, rising from 26 per cent of the total in employment in 1961 to 33 per cent in 1971, and perhaps 40 per cent in 1981.

There is no doubt that the information sector is the most rapidly growing part of the economy. The worrying question is whether it will be able to provide enough jobs in absolute terms to compensate for the jobs being lost elsewhere in the economy. To begin with, the rapidly developing technology of the information sector, notably micro-processors, is such that progressively fewer and fewer people are needed to operate it. The major impact in the 1990s is likely to be on office employment: for example, in the city of London it is estimated that it would be possible to shed a million people on the basis of the technology already available.

Another problem with the growth of work in the information sector is that, unlike the relatively smooth transformation from an agriculture-based economy to a manufacturing one 100 years ago, it does not look as though information jobs will absorb factory workers so easily: massive retraining programmes will be needed.

But, even more fundamental than this, the rate of decline of manufacturing in Britain in the early 1980s slowed growth in every other sector of the economy: the depth of Britain's recession in the years 1979–83 was so severe that even jobs in services dropped by 90,000, or 0.17 per cent.

The major employment problem confronting Britain — and for that matter all western countries — in the 1880s and 1890s is the need to devise ways of effecting a smooth transition from an industrial to an information economy — to shift labour from the manufacturing to the knowlege industries. In this endeavour the alternative approaches to the economy and employment explored in previous chapters have an essential contribution to make. Their emphasis on co-operation, protecting the environment, the small-scale and development of the local economy are generally labour-intensive and at the same time consistent with new patterns of working that are emerging in response to the demands of the expanding information sector.

The New Economics has important things to say, too, on the development of a social security system more appropriate to the re-definition of work that is underway, and on the need to decentralize government and bureaucracy in Britain to help the local economy. But before exploring these it is necessary to glance at how more flexible working patterns and attitudes to work itself are already heralding the new economy.

Merging the Formal and Informal Economies

The extraordinary characteristic of the information sector of the economy is that its growth has entailed very little automation or capital investment. For instance, the amount of investment for the average factory worker is far higher than for the average office worker, for whom a typewriter and perhaps a pocket calculator is the norm. However, as the information revolution gathers pace through the 1980s and 1990s this is likely to change radically. Growth in the information sector is difficult to project since statistics are unavailable in Britain. This is not the case in the United States where the evolving pattern is clearer, as the following projections for the country illustrate:

	1979	1990
Numbers employed in information sector (millions)	42	55
Labour cost (£ billion)	365	1250
Technology investment (£ billion)	35	240–300
Labour cost per head	£8,700	£22,730
Technology cost per head	£833	£4,360–£5,450

These figures are quoted in a pamphlet on *Networking and the Distributed Office* produced by Rank Xerox in 1984. Its authors judge that the projected increase in technology investment will have a major impact on working patterns, determined by three further factors:

● The costs of offices, and office-based functions, within companies.
● The desire by individuals to regulate their own work.
● The developments of technology which make this possible at a relatively low cost.

On the first point, the Rank Xerox study notes that management

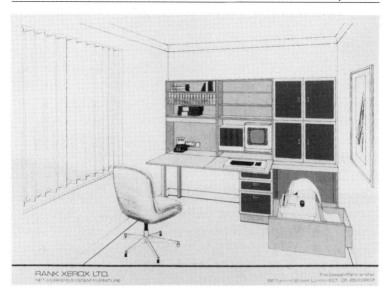

● Design for the home office, produced by Rank Xerox as part of its *Networking and the Distributed Office* scheme: an obvious way for large firms to reduce their overheads is for more and more employees to work from home, linked by a computer, and often on a freelance sub-contract basis.

has traditionally tended to regard office costs — rent, rates, light, heat, telecommunications and so on — as fixed and immutable, even though they average about a third of the outgoings of any large company. An obvious way of reducing these costs, however, is simply by employing fewer workers at a central location, by sub-contracting work to autonomous groups or individuals, and by allowing some of the workforce at least, to work from home. Certainly, the development of micro-computers and electronic mailing (computer link-ups using the telephone system) have brought the possibility within the financial reach of the smallest company. And as the authors of the Rank Xerox study remark: 'It is our contention that many individuals in today's (and, particularly, tomorrow's) better educated workforces, will seek, either in groups or as individuals, a higher measure of autonomy.'

How rapidly and to what extent are we likely to see this sort of trend developing? If the judgement of John Harvey-Jones, the chairman of ICI, is anything to go by it could happen remarkably quickly. Speaking in 1983, he concluded:

● Above is Barry Cooper, a transport consultant, who works from his Hertfordshire home — linked by computer and electronic mail to clients around the world. Barry is also the convenor of the Town and Country Information Network (TACIN). See Source Guide at the end of this chapter.

● More and more women are entering the formal economy and gaining the skills to do so — these are at the pioneering South Glamorgan Women's Workshop where unemployed women over twenty-five learn skills in basic computing, electronics and micro-electronics.

> I suppose that instead of our present UK workforce of over 50,000, we will end up with a hard core of no more than 3,000 full-time employees with many others being retained on a jobbing basis. This is the kind of thing that will have happened by the year 2010. Technology is moving in this direction and the social requirements are moving in this direction. It is therefore THE new direction.

Alongside this trend of decentralizing work, especially in the information sector, away from a single office and single employer, is a parallel one towards part-time work. It was stated earlier that women now represent 44 per cent of the workforce in Britain. What should be added is that 40 per cent of these are working part-time. Women are naturally in the forefront since part-time paid employment provides the flexibility many of them need to fit in with family commitments. Nevertheless, it is indicative of the importance of the information sector of the economy that so many women's groups throughout Britain are engaged in self-help initiatives to equip themselves to cope with computers and electronics. One example is the pioneering South Glamorgan Women's Workshop, set up in 1983 to provide vocational training for women over the age of twenty-five who wish to return to work. It is aimed at those who are unemployed or threatened with unemployment. Trainees attend the course for two-and-a-half days a week over a full year to learn skills in basic computing, electronics and micro-electronics. On the spot nursery facilities are provided for children. In the first year demand for the fifty places on the course was exceeded by 200 per cent.

One in five of Britain's workforce were working part-time in 1984 with the forecast that this would increase to one in four by 1990. For the purposes of the statistics 'part-time' work is defined as less than 30 hours per week. Yet, as the 'full-time' definition, of something around 40 hours, creeps downwards, with possibly a 35-hour week being the norm by the end of the 1990s, the distinction will become blurred. These changes form the background to a growing appreciation of the role of what is termed the 'informal economy' in which we all engage, whether it be the 'black economy' where cash is exchanged, the 'voluntary economy' — one survey in 1982 estimated that 18 million people in Britain were engaged in the voluntary sector, equivalent to 500,000 full-time workers — or the 'household economy'. Appreciation of the importance of the informal economy is directly consequent upon the increasing amount of time all of us give to it. As a result there is a slowly changing attitude to work itself, as being far more than the time we spend in an office or factory for which we are paid. Work is coming to be regarded in a more holistic way with the women's movement in the vanguard of changing attitudes. For instance, in her important study *Working Your Way to the Bottom: the feminization of poverty,* Hilda Scott quotes an article from *Radical America,* published in 1973, in which Angela Weir and Elizabeth Wilson argue that work and leisure should not be regarded as separate entities:

> What we rebel against is the separation of work from enjoyment, and of home from work. Nor do we want individual men taking over some of 'our' jobs in the home while we take over some of 'his' in the office or factory. We want greater flexibility between work and home — to have our kids with us at our place of work, or to work at home; we want greater flexibility in our concepts of what is mental and what is manual labour, and also of the nature of skills . . .

The gradual merging of the formal and informal economies

that is being predicted here is bound to be accompanied by a clash of values. Decisions in the formal economy of private industry are generally dictated by the need for profit, often at the expense of concern for social costs, and by effective demand — where about 20 per cent of the population controls more than 40 per cent of the purchasing power in Britain and most other industrialized countries. On the other hand, decisions made in the informal economy are more directly responsive to household and community needs and tend to reflect the co-operative, ecological values that typify the alternative approaches to economic activity outlined in previous chapters. At the Other Economic Summit in 1985 the Canadian economist David Ross contrasted the formal and informal economies in the following terms:

> Informal activity is associated with more face-to-face contact, both among those making decisions and those affected by them; by more concensus-type decision-making; by less specialization and stereotyping; by few regulations; by more direct attention being paid to personal development; by more flexible work routines; by increased local decision-making; by a greater reliance on self and community resources; by the benefit of production being distributed more according to need; by the absence of capital accummulation for its own sake; by the reduced emphasis placed on money; by increased direct concern for the community, the environment and the welfare of future generations; and by more co-operation.

Just to list these values might seem merely to emphasize their idealism and distance from the pressures facing the harsh competitive world of the formal economy. However, as has been discussed above, the demands of new technology and business efficiency are combining with the preferences of people to force the pace. And this is being increasingly recognized by far-sighted managers within the formal economy, as this statement from Adrian Cadbury, chairman of Cadbury Schweppes, in 1982 illustrates:

> We have to take account of the changes which are taking place in the pattern of employment and in attitudes to work . . . a blurring of traditional distinctions between full and part-time work; being in and out of employment; between work, leisure and education,

and between the formal and informal economies.

The logic of these economic and social trends will lead large firms to break their businesses down into smaller units and to move towards an organizational structure which is more like a federation of small enterprises. Two of the attributes of the small enterprise are that it can adapt rapidly to changes in the market place or in its costs, and that it buys its services in rather than providing them in-house. In a highly competitive world of slow growth, any business organized on a large-scale and with the traditional top-hamper of overheads will lose out against lower cost, more flexible rivals. I would expect to see such companies making each section of their business as independent in its operations as possible and these sections in turn will strip out any activities which are not essential for the continued survival of their own particular enterprise . . .

I see the future of manufacturing industry in particular, lying in small units, flexibly managed, largely autonomous, organized on the basis of individuals rather than departments, and based on personal contract rather than collective negotiation.

So the trends are moving in favour of small, dispersed and locally-based enterprise consistent with the thinking of the New Economics. If the trends are to be maximized there is urgent need for two major institutional reforms which are the foundations of a vision of the future in which a thriving network of autonomous but inter-connected local economies have established themselves as the conventional norm. These reforms are the need for a Basic Income and for a decentralized system of regional government in Britain.

A Basic Income

The first institutional foundation of the New Economics would weaken the link between work and cash remuneration by instituting a Basic Income scheme. The principle involved is blindingly simple; the implications enormous. All existing social security and welfare payments would be abolished and replaced with a basic income paid to every man, woman and child resident in the United Kingdom. This would provide for basic subsistence and the level would depend mainly on age. The cost of the scheme, which need be no more than that of the present system, could be met by income tax and VAT; National Insurance contributions by workers and employers alike would be unnecessary.

All income, other than the Basic Income would be taxable. Therefore, there would come a point in each person's earnings at which tax paid equals the Basic Income. This would be the *break even point,* below which the individual is a net beneficiary and above which a net contributor to the system. Most people would of course, be net contributors. The higher the Basic Income, the higher the tax rates necessary to finance the scheme. But it would be possible to pay a Basic Income at least at current rates of benefit — and higher rates for pensioners and the disabled — if all tax reliefs and allowances were taken into account and tax rates ranged from a 40 per cent starting point, rising to 45 per cent for between average and twice average earnings, and then rising progressively to 60 per cent for four times average earnings and above.

With modern technology the Basic Income could be paid automatically each week (or month) by computer into personal Giro accounts. No cheques need be sent out and no one need queue for payment. Most adults would receive the same standard amount, about equal to the present unemployment benefit for a single person, with children receiving less according to age, and the elderly more. Because the amount would depend only on age the scheme would be simple to understand and would need much less administration than present arrangements. It could be implemented progressively over a period of ten years, during which the present social security system would be gradually wound down and the tax system simplified.

The most striking feature of the Basic Income scheme, from the point of view of the transition to a new economy, would be its recognition that there is unpaid work as well as paid work — that the informal economy has a place as important as the formal. In the United Kingdom at present there are around 22 million people in paid work who create the wealth by which 56 million people live. Through its explicit recognition that there is unpaid work as well as paid work, a Basic Income scheme would show that, in fact, 34 million workers create the quality of life by which 56 million live — the 'non-workers' being 9 million elderly people and 13 million children under sixteen. The present rigid division between the 'unemployed' and the 'employed', between 'them' and 'us', between claimants and non-claimants would be relaxed. Basic incomes would restore dignity to the unemployed. There would be no more separate queues for the unemployed outside the unemployment benefit offices.

A Basic Income would help remove the stigma of unemployment and reduce the sense of isolation and loss of confidence that often accompany it.

Perhaps the most important spin-off in reducing the distinction between the formal and informal economies would be the Basic Income's role in giving women a larger measure of financial independence which is vital to equality, particularly in marital relationships. An additional advantage here would be that it would make it easier for men and women to share responsibilities for caring for elderly and disabled relatives: responsibilities which are far too often regarded as unpaid women's work at present.

As well as these fundamental but non-quantifiable gains the introduction of a Basic Income scheme would bring two very important and immediate pragmatic benefits: firstly, it would provide a much-needed reform to the present social security system which is in danger of collapsing under the weight of the sheer numbers of claimants; and, secondly, it would harness the welfare and tax system more closely to the task of creating new jobs for the unemployed.

On the first point, the fact of the matter is that the present social security system is no longer able to cope with the growth in the number of claimants, particularly the unemployed. Between the mid-1940s, when the present system came into operation under the 1942 Beveridge Plan, and the mid-1980s the number of claimants has increased by more than 400 per cent, to 12 million people. The Beveridge Plan assumed that society would be able to provide full employment. If people were out of work it would be for short periods of time only and it was on this basis that the *contributory principle* for national insurance benefit was devised. Under this principle workers make a regular contribution from their earnings in order to receive some compensation from the government if they become temporarily unemployed. And provision is made for supplementary benefit to be paid to those out of work and not entitled to unemployment benefit, as a last resort.

But large-scale and long-term unemployment has undermined the contributory principle. By the mid-1980s four million people plus their families — about seven million in all — were dependent on supplementary benefit, and a million had been out of work for more than a year. In addition, social change had brought new needs that were not anticipated in the early 1940s — the increased number of single-parent families and the increased number of elderly being only two examples.

Over the years a labyrinth of regulations have been established which has made the social security system beyond the comprehension of the majority of claimants. The range of means tested benefits steadily increased until by the mid-1980s there were some forty-five. These have helped create what is known as the poverty trap: families and individuals trapped into poverty because benefits are withdrawn at a faster rate than that at which income increases. For instance, for every extra £1 many families earn each week, they face a loss of 39p in income tax and national insurance, 17p in housing benefit, and 50p from withdrawal of Family Income Supplement — a net *loss* of 6p for every £1 earned.

Under a Basic Income scheme there would be no such threats of deduction. A person could take a part-time job *and* receive a Basic Income at the same time. At once this would remove the poverty trap, simplify the regulations, and make it easier for unemployed people to 'edge their way back' into employment through part-time work. And, in any event, as was discussed earlier in this chapter, part-time work is likely in future to become much more widespread.

This aspect leads into perhaps the greatest advantage of a Basic Income Scheme: under it industry's wage bill would fall since

● The Basic Income scheme was an important topic at the 1985 Other Economic Summit held in London as a self-conscious rival to the World Economic Summit of OECD leaders.

employers would no longer have to pay the subsistence component of income. This would provide a major new incentive for job creation on a number of fronts. First, there would be a general uplift because the wage bill to industry would be reduced. At the very least, this would protect many jobs that might otherwise be threatened. Secondly, since the number of jobs in capital-intensive manufacturing industry can be expected to decline, the main hope for future job creation on a wide scale must be in labour-intensive service industries such as leisure and social services, tourism and retailing and also in the information sector. But as we have already seen, these jobs will tend to be either part-time or poorly paid or both. So the injection of a subsistence wage element by a Basic Income Scheme into this area of the economy will be especially productive in helping create work.

A further reason why a Basic Income Scheme would help positively in job creation is because, once in place, it would reduce the need for statutory controls covering minimum wages, employment protection and compulsory redundancy payments. These can be counter-productive, for they tend to *increase* unemployment by discouraging employers from hiring new staff: they defend the jobs of the haves against the possible jobs of the have-nots. On the other hand, the protection afforded by Basic Income should make many of these controls unnecessary.

A Basic Income scheme is a practical policy today because technological advance and automation, especially in the manufacturing sector of the economy, has made it possible for great wealth to be produced by relatively few people. This change, because of the unemployment it causes, in turn makes a Basic Income scheme urgently necessary. The main impediment to its introduction is that it would be more radically redistributive of incomes than the present system. As Anne Miller, an economics lecturer at Heriot-Watt University, concluded in a paper presented to the 1985 Other Economic Summit:

> The privileged minority who are likely to face an increased tax liability by the adoption of a basic income approach, are also the vocal minority who currently hold power in many key positions in our economy, including MPs, government Ministers, high ranking civil servants, and executives of the major political parties. This minority could form a formidable opposition to plans to implement such a reform.

However, like so many of the prescriptions of the New Economics, it is likely in the end to come down to a trade-off: a choice between forgoing short-term vested interest, or facing the social instability and economic crisis that long-term mass unemployment will inevitably bring in its wake.

A Decentralized System

A central theme of the New Economics, and the thread running through this book, is the need to base economic activity on local self-reliance. All the projects surveyed in earlier chapters, whether worker co-operatives, recycling ventures, community initiatives or ecological approaches to capital formation, have this in common. Without exception they involve enterprises that tend to be small and intimately related to the local economy. And, as has been argued earlier in this chapter, current trends in new technology — the growth of the information sector and the way large-scale business is beginning to respond — all favour the small, flexible and decentralized business. Moreover, as discussed in chapter 2, this approach is especially appropriate in a country where there is so much inequality between one region and another.

In October 1985 a report produced by the North of England Regional Consortium county and district councils in the North, North-West and Yorkshire and Humberside noted that this area had lost 730,000 jobs in the previous eight years, 64 per cent of the total UK figure. Unemployment in northern Britain was more than 50 per cent higher than in southern:

> Although it is claimed that large numbers of new jobs are being created, there is no evidence that the North is receiving its fair share. In parallel with the job losses, production levels in the North are falling progressively further behind the prosperous South. The consequence of this is that unemployment has not been ameliorated by capital investment in industries in the North.

The report, *The State of the Regions,* went on to call for government resistance to pressure for more housing and industry in the South-East; support for regional airports; a commitment to examine the regional effects of spending programmes; a study of the investment policies of financial institutions and their effect on the regions; and finally, and crucially, further decentralization of government.

During 1982 a Labour Party Regional Policy Group under the chairmanship of John Prescott, MP for Hull, toured the whole of Britain before drawing up a radical set of proposals for an *Alternative Regional Strategy* for the party. Though it received little attention at the time the document was a significant milestone for a party which traditionally has put so much faith in controlling the 'commanding heights' of industry and manipulating the centralized levers of power. What was perhaps most significant was the study group's account of the more than 200 meetings it held around the country:

> The regions we visited were of two basic types: the fringe areas that have suffered from mass unemployment for many years; and the traditionally prosperous areas that are only now feeling the effects of industrial collapse. Yet despite this, one theme was stressed wherever we went, North or South, urban or rural. It was this: 'You must realize that our area is different from others'.

However, the group also observed:

> One of the most important themes we detected was a feeling of isolation in the regions. Despite massive increases in unemployment, the only recourse a region has is to central government. The time-honoured trek to London to see the Minister has now become almost meaningless, as the threshold for aid, whether in percentage or absolute terms continues to increase. As a result, communities throughout the country are demanding a greater say in the running of their own affairs. If there was one theme that came across in the consultation more than any other, it was the need to plan from the bottom up, to allow the people affected by mass unemployment to build on their own fine-grained knowledge of their area, their problems and their potential.

The study group went on to recommend the setting up of a network of democratically elected regional assemblies across the country, responsible for supervising regional development boards which would support and extend the work of local authority-based enterprise boards. In addition, the assemblies would prepare regional development plans covering the economy, environment, social services and transport, and co-ordinate other services presently provided at the regional level, such as health and water. Changes along these lines would entail a rationalization of the local government system below the new regional governments, probably establishing single-tier authorities, and a shake-up of administration at the centre. The need for many central departments such as Trade and Industry and Environment in their present form would disappear. The change would also present an opportunity for reforming the House of Lords, retaining a second chamber but making it comprise representatives of the regional governments.

The devolution policy of the Labour government in the 1970s pointed in the same direction as outlined in the *Alternative Regional Strategy,* but with one crucial difference. In the 1970s the party confined its thinking on decentralization to the benefits that would accrue in greater accountability and democratic control. In the 1980s it developed its thinking to embrace the economic benefits that decentralization would bring. These were also stressed by the newly-formed Social Democratic Party which, in a policy paper published in 1982, suggested three reasons why Assemblies for Wales, Scotland and the English regions would have 'a major impact on economic vitality':

(1) They would fill a vacuum in economic planning;
(2) They would establish new centres of power with major budgets of some 30 per cent of public spending amounting to around £35 billion; and
(3) The highlighting of inter-regional spending would benefit the poorer regions.

A further, and perhaps even more fundamental economic gain in decentralizing the political structure would be the pressure it would create for decentralizing the financial system. The simple fact is that at present Britain has, with very few exceptions, no regionally orientated financial system, public or private, which can consistently examine the needs of locally or regionally-based companies. Britain has the most centralized financial system in Europe, with all the major clearing banks, and other main financial institutions such as insurance companies, based in London. In contrast, to take just one example, West Germany has a number of strong regional banks which lend more in total to the regions than the major national banks. Furthermore, a number of banks are wholly or partly owned by the Lander, the federal West German states.

Along with moves towards a Basic Income, the creation of a decentralized political and economic system based on elected

Welsh, Scottish and English Regional Assemblies would provide the essential foundations for the evolution of the New Economics.

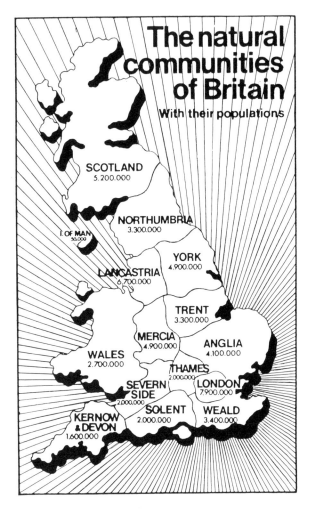

One scheme for decentralization to the regions of England, Scotland and Wales.

This map is taken from the author's 1974 volume *The Centralist Enemy*. For a detailed discussion of the issues involved see the report of the Royal Commission on the Constitution 1969–1973, and particularly its Memorandum of Dissent — Cmd. 5460, available from HMSO.

The division of England into regions is, of course, a major problem, but the map indicates the possibilities.

A Vision of the Future

As has been outlined in this chapter the New Economics has a broad vision of a decentralized, small-scale, co-operative and ecologically-orientated society in which maximum emphasis is placed on the local economy. Economic policy and political organization should enable people and the communities in which they live to be more self-reliant, to meet a larger proportion of local needs from local work and local resources. The idea of work itself should be broadened to include as far as possible living as a whole, so that the present sharp differentiation between paid employment and the rest of life's activity can be reduced.

But the New Economics is not just another economic theory. The account of it given in this book demonstrates that its holistic approach to life is worked out in action, whether in a worker's co-operative, a recycling project, or developing a more ecological attitude towards investment. This book has only touched on a few examples of what is happening around Britain. One final case is the Lightmoor Project, a new settlement being developed

● Some of the members of the Lightmoor Project, pictured in the summer of 1985 as the first turf was being cut. In the centre is Tony Gibson who forsees a resurgence of cottage industries aided by high technology.

on a 250-acre site at the edge of Telford New Town in Shropshire. It is a deliberate effort to create from scratch a more self-reliant community to fit in with the way the economy as a whole is moving. The first turf was cut in the summer of 1985 with three families moving on to the first 23 acres of the site to build their own homes, according to their own design. Eventually it is hoped that a dozen families will occupy this area, giving them enough space to create smallholdings. The people developing the site envisage working in conventionally paid employment for about half of their time, the rest being spent on self-sustaining activity. The founder of the scheme, Tony Gibson, a development officer with the Town and Country Planning Association, believes that large-scale industry is in inescapable decline; in its place he sees a resurgence of cottage industries aided by high technology:

> It is no longer necessary to crowd everything together in an industrial slum or to spread everything out in ribbon development that lacerates the countryside. The neighbourhood of the future, as it could be realized in Lightmoor, might be made up of a few small clusters of houses, market gardens and workshops, separated by open country and woodland.

The vision of the New Economics explored in this book may appear at times hopelessly idealistic, even fanciful, in the face of continuing mass unemployment and industrial decline. But when examined on the ground, in its practice, its approach can be seen as hard-headed, practical commonsense. And its adherents are growing. It is estimated, for instance, that in Britain today there are some five million people paying subscriptions to environmental organizations.

The growth of the New Economy is an evolutionary process: its projects and activities gradually filling the spaces left by the cracking of the old order. The New Economics does not offer a theoretical blueprint for the future; its very essence is to rely on the integrity and initiative of communities working out their own salvation. What the New Economics does offer is a global ecological concern combined with practical local action. It is our best hope for work in the future.

Source Guide

Two outstanding treatments of current changes in the economy and the future outlook are Tom Stonier's *The Wealth of*

Information — *a Profile of Post-Industrial Society* (Methuen, 1983) and Charles Handy's *The Future of Work* (Basil Blackwell, 1984). A useful perspective is provided by Andre Gorz, *Farewell to the Working Class* (Pluto, 1982) and a more apocalyptic vision by Alvin Toffler's *The Third Wave* (Pan, 1981). The New Economics are placed in a wider ecological perspective by Jonathan Porritt's *Seeing Green* (Basil Blackwell, 1984).

Networking — *The distributed office, a new venture in modes of employment* can be obtained by writing to Phil Judkins, Rank Xerox House, 338 Euston Road, London NW1 3BH. A useful background to the emerging informal economy is Jonathan Gershuny's *After Industrial Society? The Emerging Self-Service Economy* (Macmillan, 1976). An overview from an American perspective is provided by Paul Hawken's *The Next Economy* (Angus and Robertson, 1983). A British view on how new technology is going to shape our lives is Shirley Williams' *A Job To Live* — *The Impact of Tomorrow's Technology on Work and Society* (Penguin, 1985).

For a woman's perspective Hilda Scott's *Working Your Way to the Bottom* — *the feminization of poverty* (Pandora, an imprint of Routledge and Kegan Paul, 1984) is outstanding and contains a comprehensive bibliography. The South Glamorgan Women's Workshop can be contacted at Edena House, East Canal Wharf, Cardiff, CF1 5QQ. An excellent discussion of the informal economy, especially as it affects women, is contained in Ivan Illich's *Shadow Work* (Marion Boyars, 1981).

For more information on Basic Income, contact Peter Ashby, Secretary, Basic Income Research Group, 26 Bedford Square, London WC1. The group, which operates under the wing of the National Council for Voluntary Organizations, publishes a regular bulletin on its activities. Peter Ashby has written a short pamphlet arguing the case for a Basic Income scheme entitled *Social Security After Beveridge* — *What Next?*

The State of the Regions report is obtainable from the North of England Regional Consortium, PO Box 532, Town Hall, Manchester M60 2LA. The most comprehensive study of the issues so far as England is concerned is *Regional Government in England,* edited by Brian Hogwood and Michael Keating (Clarendon Press, 1982). A different perspective is contained in Tom Nairn's *The Break-Up of Britain* — *Crisis and Neo-Nationalism* (New Left Books, 1977). An ongoing and comprehensive study of the issues is made by the Centre for the Study of Public Policy,

University of Strathclyde, Glasgow G1 1XQ which will provide a list of more than 100 papers it has published over the past decade.

The Lightmoor Project, at the edge of Telford New Town, offers scope for community-minded individuals and families to set up their own homes and cottage industries (craft or hi-tech) with mortgage finance, and help plan their neighbourhood on co-operative lines. For details, write to The Town and Country Planning Association, 17 Carlton House Terrace, London SW1Y 5AS. A similar project is the Greentown Project in Milton Keynes. Details are available from The Greentown Group, c/o Urban Studies Centre, 553 Silbury Boulevard, Milton Keynes MK9 3AR. The Town and Country Information Network is developing a computerized database on a wide range of information sources for community development. Subscribers can choose to have access to the information by means of a quarterly *Index,* or instantaneously, via electronic mail. Contact Barry Cooper, TACIN, Upper Butts, Orcop, Herefordshire.

Index